W9-DJL-346

# SOCIETIES:
# A MULTI-CULTURAL
# READER

# SOCIETIES: A MULTI-CULTURAL READER

to accompany

Alex Thio's Sociology: A Brief Introduction

Third Edition

Peter B. Morrill

Bronx Community College

of the City University of New York

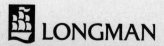 LONGMAN

SOCIETIES: A Multicultural Reader to accompany Thio, SOCIOLOGY: A Brief Introduction

Copyright © 1997 Addison-Wesley Educational Publishers Inc.

All rights reserved.  Printed in the United States of America.  No part of this book may be used or reproduced in any manner whatsoever without written permission from the publisher except, testing materials may be copied for classroom use.  For information, address Addison Wesley Educational Publishers Inc., 10 East 53rd Street, New York, NY 10022.

ISBN: 0-673-98114-2

96  97  98  99  00  9  8  7  6  5  4  3  2  1

# Preface

This book of thirty-eight readings accompanies SOCIOLOGY: A Brief Introduction, 3rd Edition, by Alex Thio. Its purpose is to further illustrate the text's concepts so that students can fully explore the diversity of American culture and other societies. The reader contains two or three selections for each chapter of the text. They are divided between descriptions of an American subculture or group and accounts of social life in another society. In addition, each reading begins with a short introduction that relates the material to key concepts in the text.

I have also provided students with a "resource page" for each chapter's set of readings. This page includes study questions and a list of key concepts for each reading. I have also provided a list of additional books related to the reading which provides sources for more reading or the beginnings of a term paper or book report.

I have selected articles that will provide students with interesting descriptions of diverse sub-cultures and groups. The articles come from a wide variety of sources, including magazines like <u>Society</u>, <u>Smithsonian</u>, and <u>The New Republic</u>, and many recently published books.

The readings can be used in several ways. They can help stimulate classroom discussion. They can become the basis of student review or exam questions, especially through the use of each reading's study questions. They can also help students explore some of the major changes underway in America and throughout the world. The reader contains articles on such key international issues as changes in the Soviet Union, the destruction of the Amazon jungle, the Islamic Revolution, and important domestic concerns like racial and ethnic conflict and changes in the economy.

I would like to thank Tom Kulesa and Alan McClare of Addison Wesley Longman for their many suggestions and careful guidance.

JULY, 1996                                                                    PETER B. MORRILL

# Student Introduction

This reader, which accompanies Alex Thio's SOCIOLOGY: A Brief Introduction, 3rd Edition, is designed to help you understand a range of sociological concepts through examples of diverse cultural groups in the United States and other countries. The text introduces you to the sociological perspective and a wide variety of concepts sociologists use to describe human behavior. This reader, in turn, provides a rich set of examples of various cultures that will help you apply the concepts found in the text.

The theme that runs through all 38 readings is how sociology helps us understand the diversity of human behavior. This theme is reflected in readings such as Chapter 15's "The Global Tide" and Chapter 2's "Protecting Cultures." I have included readings on specific cultural groups such as Puerto Rican women from Chicago and Japanese children. These readings, which come from many sources, show how diverse peoples live, how societies like America and the Hong Kong are changing, and how to understand other ways of life.

Here are some suggestions for how to use this reader to better understand the concepts of sociology:

• Before looking at the reading, study the related chapter in the textbook and review relevant lecture notes. You will better understand the lives of people described in the reading if you have a grasp of basic concepts.

• Read the short introductions provided at the beginning of each reading. These introductions are designed to link the text's concepts to the selection and to help you focus your reading.

• Read each article thoroughly. The selections are short and interesting, and you should be able to read them with little difficulty.

• Use the Resource Page provided for each chapter's set of readings. Here, write down your answers to the study questions provided for each reading. These questions are designed to help you summarize each reading's main ideas and to apply the related sociological concepts to them. Also, define the list of key concepts provided and read more about the groups discussed in the readings.

Sociology can greatly help us understand the ways of mankind and I hope you will successfully use this reader to gain this important skill of sociological analysis.

# Contents

# SOCIETIES:
# A MULTI-CULTURAL
# READER

# A. In Defence of Sociology

ANTHONY GIDDENS

*Sociology has lost some of its appeal since the 1960s as reformers of society have taken legal and political, rather than academic, routes to social reform and the discipline has split into many specialities. Several articles and books have attacked the field and enrollment in sociology courses has declined. However, sociology's mission, which originated in the Industrial Revolution, remains strong. Anthony Giddens, a leading sociologist, argues that sociology continues to provide knowledge for modern society.*

There's something about sociology that raises hackles that other academic subjects fail to reach. Economics may be the dismal science, full of jargon that few can understand and seemingly irrelevant to the practical tasks of economic life. But sociology is often indicted on all counts—diffuse and lacking a coherent subjectmatter, as well as being jargon-ridden. What do you get when you cross a sociologist with a member of the mafia? An offer you can't understand.

What is it with sociology? Why is it so irritating to so many? Some sociologists might answer ignorance; others fear. Why fear? Well, because many sociologists like to think of their subject as a dangerous and discomfiting one. Sociology, they are prone to say, is an intrinsically subversive subject: it challenges our assumptions about ourselves as individuals and about the wider social contexts in which we live. And in the 1960s, for many people the heyday of sociology, the discipline seemed to live up to this firebrand reputation. In truth, however, even in the 1960s and early 1970s, sociology wasn't intrinsically associated with the left, let alone with the revolutionaries.

Sociology has currently been going through a hard time in the very country where it has long been most well developed, the U.S. A prominent American sociologist, Irving Louis Horowitz, recently published a book entitled *The Decomposition of Sociology*, a work which he says was "more a matter of pain rather than pride to have felt the need to write." The discipline, he says, has gone sour. Sociology has largely become the home of the discontented, a gathering of groups with special agendas, from the proponents of gay rights to liberation theology. Sociology is decomposing partly because it has come to be just what its critics always took it to be, a pseudo-science; and because there has been

*Excerpted from Anthony Giddens, "In Defence of Sociology," NEW STATESMAN AND SOCIETY, March 20, 1995, pp. 33-34. Reprinted with permission of New Statesman and Society.*

an outflow of respectable, empirically-oriented social scientists into other, more narrowly defined areas such as urban planning, demography, criminology or jurisprudence.

Let's deal first of all with the old chestnut that sociology doesn't have a proper field of investigation. The truth of the matter is that the field of study of sociology, as understood by the bulk of its practitioners, is no more, but no less, clearly defined than that of any other academic discipline. Consider, for example, history. There's an obvious subject matter there, it would seem—the past. But the past embraces everything! No clear or bounded field of study here, and history as an academic discipline is every bit as riven by methodological disputes about its true nature as sociology ever has been.

Sociology is a generalising discipline that concerns itself above all with modernity—with the character and dynamics of modern or industrialised societies. It shares many o fits methodological strategies—and problems—not only with history, but with the whole gamut of the social sciences. The more empirical issues it deals with are very real. Of all the social sciences, sociology bears most directly on the issues that concern us in our everyday lives—the development of modern urbanism, crime and punishment, gender, the family, religion, social and economic power.

Given that sociological research and thinking is more or less indispensable in contemporary society, why has the subject so often attracted the criticism that it is unenlightening—that it is common sense wrapped up in somewhat unattractive jargon? Although specific pieces of research could always be questioned, it would be difficult to argue that there was no point in carrying out, say, comparative studies of the incidence of divorce in different countries. Sociologists engage in all sorts of research which, once one has some sense of them, would prove interesting, and be thought important, by most reasonably neutral observers.

There is, however, another, more subtle reason why sociology may appear quite often to proclaim what is in any case obvious to common sense. This is that social research doesn't, and can't, remain separate from the social world it describes. Social research forms so much a part of our consciousness today that we take it for granted. But all of us depend upon such research for what we regard as common sense—as "what everyone knows." Everyone knows, for example, that divorce rates are high in today's society; yet such "obvious knowledge," of course, depends upon regular social research, whether it happens to be carried out by government researchers or academic sociologists.

These considerations, obviously, don't help with the issue of whether sociology as an academic discipline is in a state of sorry decline or even dissolution since its heyday in the 1960s, if that period was indeed its apogee. Things *have* changed in sociology over the past 30 years, but not all for the worse. For one thing, the centre of power has shifted. American sociology used to dominate world sociology, but it does so no longer. Especially so fars as sociological theorising is concerned, the centre of gravity has shifted elsewhere, particularly to Europe. The major sociological thinkers now are over here rather than over there.

Sociology in the U.S. appears to have become over-professionalized, with research groups concentrating on their own patches, having little knowledge of, or interest in, anyone else's. Everyone in U.S. sociology has a "field" and whatever speciality it happens to be effectively defines his or her identity. Quantrophrenia is rife in American sociology departments. For many, if you can't count it, it doesn't count; the result, to say the least, can be a certain lack of creativity.

There is a good deal of sense in William Julius Wilson's exhortation to sociologists to engage in research immediately relevant to public policy issues and to participate forcefully in the wide debates their work may arouse. After all, many of the questions raised in the political arena are sociological—questions to do, for instance, with welfare, crime or the family. Sociological work is relevant, not just to their formulation as particular types of policy questions, but to grasping the likely consequences of whatever policies might be initiated in relation to them.

But recommending sociology to a public policy making agenda wouldn't address the other issues raised about the so-called decline of sociology? It is a discipline without a common conceptual core, in danger of breaking up into unconnected specialities? And have the most innovative authors moved elsewhere? Most important of all, perhaps, has it lost its cutting edge?

Everything in the sociological garden certainly isn't rosy—although was it ever? Funding for social research has dropped off sharply since the early 1970s—there isn't the scale of empirical work there once was. But it would be difficult to argue that sociology is off the pace intellectually, especially if one broadens the angle again and moves back to a more international perspective. Most of the debates that grab the intellectual headlines across the social sciences, and even the humanities, today carry a strong sociological input. Sociological authors have pioneered discussions of postmodernism, the post-industrial or information society, globalisation, the transformation of everyday life, gender and sexuality, the changing nature of work and the family, the "underclass" and ethnicity.

You might still ask: what does it all add up to? And here indeed there is a lot of sociological work to be done. Some of that work has to be investigatory or empirical, but some must be theoretical. More than any other intellectual endeavour, sociological reflection is central to grasping the social forces remaking our lives today. Social life has become episodic, fragmentary and dogged with new uncertainties, which it must be the business of creative sociological thought to help us understand better.

Sociology should rehone its cutting edge, as neoliberalism disappears into the distance along with orthodox socialism. Some questions to which we need new answers have a perennial quality, while others are dramatically new. Tackling these, as in previous times, calls for a healthy dose of what C. Wright Mills famously called the sociological imagination. Sociologists, don't despair! You still have a world to win, or at least interpret.

# B. Interviewing and Cultural Identity

MIRI SONG AND DAVID PARKER

*One of sociology's most widely used research techniques is the face-to-face interview. Sociologists are trained to develop a set of careful questions and to conduct interviews in a neutral way so as to make the research as objective as possible. However, the interviewer's cultural, class and gender background can influence a subject's response to questions and how the researcher interprets responses. This reading explores the issue of the interviewer's cultural identity and shows how it can dramatically shape an interview.*

The last few decades have witnessed a notable growth in literature addressing the politics and ethics of social research. Much of this literature has addressed the importance of sensitizing researchers to the difficulties and dilemmas encountered in social research crossing sex, class, and race boundaries. There has been growing attention to the actual 'doing' of research, particularly open-ended, in-depth interviews.

Suprisingly little attention has been given to how the cultural identities of researchers may shape the research situations of ethnic minority researchers interviewing persons of the same or partially shared racial and/or ethnic background. This article has evolved out of some common concerns and experiences we had as two independent researchers on the lives of young Chinese people in Britain. As a male researcher of Chinese and British descent (David) and a female Korean-American researcher (Miri), we were struck by a number of common themes and issues which arose for us in our respective research projects. We both felt that existing scholarship on research methodology did not adequately address our own research experiences.

What issues arise, and what difficulties and/or advantages are there for the researcher who shares some racial and/or ethnic commonality with the interviewee? In this article, we aim to demonstrate how complex positionings occur throughout the interview process, by providing some examples of our respective interview experiences. We use the term 'positionings' to suggest the potentially unstable and shifting nature of the relationship between the researcher and the interviewee where they share some racial and/or ethnic commonality.

David: My own study involved extensive inter-

*Excerpted from Miri Song and David Parker, "Commonality, Difference and the Dynamics of Disclosure in In-Depth Interviewing," SOCIOLOGY, May 1995, pp. 241-256.*

views with fifty-four young Chinese people throughout Britain, and addressed their life experiences and sense of cultural identity. Interviews were reached in the main through a self-completion postal questionnaire; those who consented on the form were contacted and then interviewed face to face. Many people received survey forms from me in person in the Chinatown areas of Britain. Connecting my visual appearance to my English surname usually enabled respondents to guess in advance that I was of dual heritage. However, others wrote back, asking, 'Are you Chinese, or what?' Where my racial identity was not apparent it unfolded in the research process itself, often through letters.

One of my most immediate experiences with the interviewees was that young Chinese people who strongly defined themselves as Chinese, often did so in contrast to me. This also occurred more indirectly through revealing their perception of what a part-Chinese person's identity was-'mixed up' or a 'problem.' One person who knew of my dual heritage background said, 'If you say your identity is neither one nor the other, you will find there is a bit of a lack', and later in the discussion looked me piercingly in the face and stated: 'If one hasn't got his or her own cultural identity, he or she will feel really lost one day in the future, if not yet...' Clearly, my assumed confusion and ambivalence regarding my cultural identity was being used to buttress the interviewee's strength in being Chinese.

Those with strongly held Chinese identities were also keen to establish 'how Chinese are you?', 'can you speak Chinese?', or 'was your father or your mother English'? It was usually made clear that I had been taken as very English and that I was being talked to as if I was an English person.

Experiences of commonality were assumed by those who, like myself, had grown up in particular urban areas of Britain and experienced racial harassment. The positioning of me as someone 'totally English', particularly by those anxious to assert their sense of being Chinese, could be suspended when shared experiences of discrimination were being discussed.

What my research demonstrated was the complexity of these identifications and disidentifications; so many dimension of sameness and difference can be operating at any given moment. And where two people may claim commonality on one dimensions, they may fall apart on another.

Miri: My research examined the labor participation of young people in Chinese take-away businesses in Britain, and focused upon their often ambivalent experiences of 'helping out'. I conducted semi-structured in-depth interviews with Chinese young people in twenty-five families, most of whom resided in the greater London area.

The relationships which developed between me and the interviewees were characterized by a persistent tension between feelings of commonality and of difference regarding our cultural identities, in spite of the fact that my research did not directly focus upon issues of cultural identity. I had not anticipated the extent to which interviewees' assumptions and perceptions of me and my cultural identity, would shape the course of interviews.

When I started my field work, I did claim some commonality as a strategy for access. As someone of Korean heritage, who had been raised in the U.S., I had anticipated that my being Korean-American, rather than Chinese, would limit access to Chinese families; in fact, I had considerable difficulty in recruiting, primarily due to concerns around privacy and trust. When I approached people about participating in the study, I was often asked why I wanted to study Chinese families in Britain. Although my own family had been privileged as immigrants, I spoke of my own experiences growing up in the U.S., where I felt some kinship with other East-Asian groups.

My being Korean-American, and what that meant to the interviewees, was often the basis for assumptions of both commonality and difference with me throughout the interview process. Interviewees' assumptions about my cultural identity were central in shaping what respondents chose to disclose to me, as well as the manner in which interviewees disclosed information about themselves. Throughout the interviews, it often seemed that the interviewees and I were 'circling' each other on certain aspects

of our cultural identities—issues which were related to our discussions about working with one's family in a Chinese take-away. This 'circling' was due to concerns about disclosing and justifying certain markers of cultural identity. It seemed that both interviewees and I were concerned about being judged by the other: how Korean or Chinese, as opposed to American or British, were we perceived to be? Feelings of defensiveness or nervousness were engendered by fears that we were seen as not Korean or Chinese 'enough.'

In our research experiences with young Chinese people, we were both surprised by the extent to which our own cultural identities as researchers were either directly or indirectly questioned or commented upon by respondents. More attention should be given to how assumptions made by interviewees regarding the cultural identity of the researcher is a crucial factor in shaping the interview process. Such assumptions shaped interviewees' accounts in that: interviewees may withhold or disclose certain kinds of information, depending upon their assumptions of the researcher; interviewees might describe aspects of their lives and their identities in terms which compare themselves to assumptions about the research.

Markers of cultural identity, such as language fluency, physical appearance, and one's personal relationships, can be the bases for claims of either commonality or difference. In addition, gender and the language in which the interview is conducted, are important in structuring not only what may be revealed in interviewees' accounts, but also the way in which information is revealed. We would argue that *multiple* positionings and (dis)identifications, which shift during the interview process, rather than a unitary sense of identity, occur in the course of an interview. It is only through the illustration of how identifications and dis-identifications actually occur in specific moments of interviews, that some of the debates about cultural identity and the research process can move ahead.

# Resource Page

## A. IN DEFENCE OF SOCIOLOGY

### Study Questions

• What are some of the problems currently facing sociology?
• How do the separate perspectives on society contribute to some of sociology's current problems?
• Why does the author feel that sociology is more than common sense?
• Why is sociological research and thinking "more or less indispensable" in modern society?
• How might sociology better meet the criticisms directed toward it?

### Key Concepts

consciousness
public policy
social problems
social research
sociology

### Additional Resources

• Anthony Giddens. *Social Theory and Modern Sociology*. Stanford, CA: Stanford University Press, 1987. A good summary of the state of modern sociological work.
• Charles Lemert. *Sociology After the Crisis*. New York: Westview, 1995. An excellent overview of sociology's problems.
• C. Wright Mills. *The Sociological Imagination*. New York: Grove Press, 1961. This classic originally identified many of sociology's current problems.
• Stephen Park Turner and Jonathan H. Turner. *The Impossible Science: An Institutional Analysis of American Sociology*. Newbury Park, CA: Sage, 1990. A good treatment.
• Ted Vaughan, Gideon Sjoberg and Larry Reyonds.
*A Critique of Contemporary Sociology*. Dix Hill,
New York: General-Hall, 1993. A good view.

## B. INTERVIEWING AND CULTURAL IDENTITY

### Study Questions

• What special situation was created by the Song and Parker's ethnic identities?
• Why did each interviewer's ethnic identity create research problems during their interviewing?
• How did the experience of these two researchers illustrate some of the methods of social research?
• How did the researchers try to achieve more objectivity in their work?
• What did the experiences of the researchers tell us about the problems of sociology as a science?

### Key Concepts

commonality
cultural identity
interviewer
positioning
research ethics

### Additional Resources

• Earl Babbie. *Observing Ourselves: Essays in Social Research*, Belmont, CA: Wadsworth Company, 1986. Excellent research essays.
• Kenneth Hoover and Todd Donovan. *The Elements of Social Scientific Thinking*, 6th Edition. New York: St. Martin's Press, 1995. A classic text on research.
• Theodore Kennedy. *You Gotta Deal With It*. New York: Oxford University Press, 1980. A fascinating book on the adventures of an African American researcher in the South.
• Paul D. Reynolds. *Ethics and Social Science Research*. Englewood Cliffs, NJ: Prentice-Hall, 1982. A basic text.
• William K. Whyte. *Participant Observation*.

# A. The Limits of Cultural Diversity

HARLEN CLEVELAND

*Televison and travel may have made every culture available to others, but this spread of awareness has not led to more tolerance of different cultures. Instead, civil war, racism and violence have often marked the relationships between cultures. This reading explores some reasons why cultural diversity has led to major problems throughout the world. The author argues that cultural diversity is limited and that we must uphold the ideal of civilization.*

I'm engaged just now in an effort to think through the most intellectually interesting, and morally disturbing, issue in my long experience of trying to think hard about hard subjects. I call it "The Limits of Cultural Diversity." If that seems obscure, wait a moment.

After the multiple revolutions of 1989, it began to look as if three ideas we have thought were Good Things would be getting in each other's way, which is not a Good Thing. What I have called the "triple dilemma," or "trilemma," is the mutually damaging collision of individual human rights, cultural human diversity, and global human opportunities. Today the damage from that collision is suddenly all around us.

In 1994, in the middle of Africa, ethnicity took over as an exclusive value, resulting in mass murder by machete. In ex-Yugoslavia (and too many other places), gunpowder and rape accomplish the same purpose: trampling on human rights and erasing human futures. Even on the Internet, where individuals can now join global groups that are not defined by place-names or cordoned off by gender or ethnicity, people are shouting at each other in flaming, capital-letters rhetoric.

Look hard at your home town, at the nearest inner city; scan the world by radio, TV, or newspapers and magazines. What's happened is all too clear: just when individual human rights have achieved superstar status in political philosophy, just when can-do information technologies promise what the U.N. Charter calls "better standards of life in larger freedom," culture and diversity have formed a big, ugly boulder in the road called Future. But is "cultural diversity" really the new Satan in our firmament? Or does it just seem so because "culture" is being used as an instrument of repression, exclusion, and extinction?

*Excerpted from Harlan Cleveland, "The Limits of Cultural Diversity," THE FUTURIST, March-April 1995, pp. 23-25. Reprinted with permission of The Futurist.*

In today's disordered world, the collision of cultures with global trends is in evidence everywhere. Ethnic nations, fragmented faiths, transnational business, and professional groups find both their inward loyalties and their international contacts leading them to question the political structures by which the world is still, if tenuously, organized. The results are sometimes symbolic and sometimes broken mosaics like the human tragedy in what used to be Yugoslavia.

More people moved in 1994 than ever before in world history, driven by fear of guns or desire for more butter and more freedom. This more mobile world multiplies the incentives for individuals to develop "multiple personalities," to become "collages" of identities, with plural loyalties to overlapping groups. Many millions of people believe that their best haven of certainty and security is a group based on ethnic similarity, common faith, economic interest, or political like-mindedness.

Societies based on fear of outsiders tend toward "totalitarian" governance. Fear pushes the culture beyond normal limits on individuals' behavior. "To say that you're ready to die for cultural identity," said one of my colleagues, "means that you're also ready to kill for cultural identity." Said another, "The ultimate consequence of what's called 'cultural identity' is Hutus and Tutsis murdering each other."

The fear that drives people to cleave to their primordial loyalties makes it harder for them to learn to be tolerant of others who may be guided by different faiths and loyalties. But isolating oneself by clinging to one's tribe is far from a stable condition; these days, the tribe itself is highly unstable. Differences in birth rates and pressures to move will continue to mix populations together. So ethnic purity isn't going to happen, even by forcible "cleansing."

Besides, cultures keep redefining themselves by mixing with other cultures, getting to know people who look, act, and believe differently. In today's more-open electronic world, cultures also expose themselves to new faiths and fashions, new lifestyles, workways, technologies, clothing, and cuisines.

The early stage of every realization of "cultural identity," every assertion of a newfound "right" of differences, does create a distinct group marked by ethnic aspect ("black is beautiful"), gender ("women's lib"), religion ("chosen people"), or status as a political minority. But when members of a group insisting on the group's uniqueness do succeed in establishing their own personal right to be different, something very important happens: They begin to be treated individually as equals and tend to integrate with more inclusive communities.

The problem does not seem to be culture itself, but cultural overenthusiasm. Cultural loyalties, says one European, have the makings of a runaway nuclear reaction. Without the moderating influence of civil society—acting like fuel rods in a nuclear reactor—the explosive potential gets out of hand. What's needed is the counterforce of wider views, global perspectives, and more universal ideas.

Post-communist societies, says a resident of one of them, have experienced a loss of equilibrium, a culture shock from the clash of traditional cultures, nostalgia for the stability of Soviet culture, and many new influences from outside. What's needed, he thinks, is cultural richness without cultural dominance, but with the moderating effect of interculural respect.

We have inherited a fuzzy vocabulary that sometimes treats culture as a synonym for civilization. In this construct, civilization is what's universal—values, ideas, and practices that are in general currency everywhere, either because they are viewed as objectively "true" or because they are accepted pragmatically as useful in the existing circumstances. These accepted "truths" offer the promise of weaving together a civitas of universal laws and rules, becoming the basis for a global civil society.

If civilization is what's universal, culture is the substance and symbols of the community. Culture meets the basic human need for a sense of belonging, for participating in the prides and fears that are shared with an in-group. Civilization is rooted in compromise—between the idea of a democratic state and a strong state, between a free-market economy and a caring economy, between "open" and "closed" processes, between horizontal and vertical relationships, between active and passive citizenship. The required solvent for civilization is respect for differences. Or, we need to learn how to be different together. Civilization will be built by cooperation and compassion, in a social climate in which people in differing groups can deal with each other in ways that can also respect their cultural differences.

# B. Widowhood in South Africa

MAMPHELA RAMPHETE

*Status is a social position and roles are expectations of what individuals should do in accordance with a particular status. Sometimes, playing a role creat strain when a person has emotional or personal problems living up the expectations of a status. These concepts are fully illustrated by this reading on political funerals among black African revolutionaries in South Africa. Here, widows of men slain in the struggle for freedom must conform to the status of revolutionary widow by participating in public, political funderals despite experiencing great personal grief.*

Widowhood sweeps women into a liminal phase in which the woman's tie to the departed spouse is publicly reenacted: "The widow in mourning having lost her spouse and yet still considered married is in a special kind of ambiguous, transitional state typically involving pollution and related beliefs." The widow becomes the embodiment of loss and pain occasioned by the sting of death, and her body is turned into a focus of attention, as both subject and object of mourning rituals. The individual suffering of a widow is made social, and her body becomes a metaphor for suffering.

This essay will examine the transposition of the widow from the role of enacting and embodying personal loss to that of incorporating public loss. Political widowhood raises questions of importance about pain and suffering as social phenomena, and the extent to which social space is created or denied for the public expression of pain, loss, and suffering of individual social actors.

A widow expresses her liminal status in a variety of ways, depending on local custom: these may include eating with her left hand, wearing clothes inside out, wearing one shoe, or eating out of a lid instead of a plate. The prescription of social intercourse finds expression in widows being bound to stay at home, except for essential business trips, for which they would have to be accompanied and precautions taken to prevent them from polluting the unwary. Widows are prohibited from participation in public ceremonies and celebrations.

But political widowhood incorporates, elevates, and tranforms some of the elements of the ritual dangers emboided in personal widowhood. Individual pain and loss is claimed and given a public voice. Thus, ritual danger is contained and transformed into ritual power. By sharing the

*Excerpted from Mamphela Ramphete, "Political Widowhood in South Africa: The Embodiment of Ambiguity," DAEDALUS, Winter, 1996, pp. 99-117.*

pain with the widow and her family, the circle is widened to incorporate "the political family," represented by the political formation to which the deceased belonged. The enlarged family circle brings with it resources and corresponding responsibilities and obligations.

The acknowledgement of the pain and loss of social actors is a profoundly political act. Not all widows are acknowledged as political widows, nor are all political widows "widows." The term "political widowhood" reflects the appropriation of certain women's bodies as part of the symbolic armor mobilized by political movements in the contest for moral space following the fall of heroes in the struggle for power.

The loss of one's partner and spouse is profoundly personal. It remains deeply etched in one's psyche and soul, defying attempts to give it an escape route through the sound of wailing or words of grief. The pain of the loss of a life partner becomes incorporated in the body of the surviving spouse, sometimes becoming inaccessible even to the sufferer.

The very nature of mourning rituals makes for little personal space, as family and friends rally around to lend support and share the pain and grief. Such support is a source of great strength for the affected person. Philippe Aries has lucidly explicated the importance of mourning as a social phenomenon and the vital role of the support offered by others in acknowledgment of one's loss. But he also points to the fact that helping the survivor was neither the sole nor primary purpose of mourning: "Mourning expressed the anguish of a community that had been visited by death, contaminated by its presence, weakened by the loss of one of its members."

Thus, the meaning behind the communal support bereaved families receive is ambiguous. In focusing on the woundedness of the community, the bereaved individual may become simply part of the "ritual exercises," totally devoid of spontaneity. Thus, the individual would have little space to come to terms with her personal loss, and the process of healing would be delayed.

The enlargement of the circle of mourners to incorporate tile body politic to which the deceased also belonged brings both added support and tension. Political formations naturally want to make as much political capital as possible out of the death of a comrade. Tile funeral becomes a form of political theater that has to be managed to achieve the desired outcomes for the political formation involved. Inevitably, problems arise in balancing the wishes of the family and the desires of the politicians.

The profile desired by politicians may create tensions for the family. For example, during the height of the civil war in mid-1980s in South Africa, many families were dragged into mass political funerals against their will. They wanted to put their dead to rest without further pain, given the violent and shocking nature of the deaths of their loved ones. They also feared being caught in the cross fire between "the comrades" and the Apartheid security forces, which often ensured that mourners ended up having to run for their lives without finishing the final rites for their loved ones. On the other hand, mourners feared displeasing or defying "the comrades," who felt that it was the duty of the mourners to use every available means to advance the struggle and did not approve of any retreat from such awesome tasks. The staging of mass political funerals assumed enormous significance as opportunities to put the evil and brutality of the state in full public view. The more coffins one could line up, the stronger the message that could be communicated in this regard.

The desire for privacy by the bereaved often goes unheeded; if anything, it invites even greater attention because of the fear that, if left alone, the bereaved may become more vulnerable to contemplating undesirable and desperate actions. It is not uncommon for those sharing grief with the widow in South Africa teo engage in endless chatter intended to make light of the moment and to temporarily take her mind off graver thoughts.

The political funeral ceremony signals a widow's entry into the public arena. The desired public profile of the widow is carefully nurtured and managed. This management includes her mourning clothes, which, while communicating grief, must also communicate dignity. The politi-cal widow, unlike other widows, does not wear the symbols of ambiguity in the form of cheap clothes worn inside out, or one sloe; the shaven head is replaced by carefully groomed hair and an appropriate hat.

The negotiation of the public space after the funeral involves a number of issues. The label of "political" widow carries with it public ownership of the person of the widow. She becomes a valuable resource for the political organization to which her husband and/or herself were affiliated. She embodies the social memory that has to be cultivated and kept alive to further the goals of the struggle, and hopefully to also act as a deterrent against further losses such as hers. She also becomes the embodiment of the brutality of the state, which leaves women like her in a vulnerable, liminal state.

There are too many individuals, families, and communities whose pain remains unacknowledged. The definition of "tile political" as opposed to "the personal" is in itself a political question. Political widows who are victims of forced removals, random killings, or industrial accidents are as deserving as any other of making claims for historical wrongs done to them. Their private suffering needs to be made visible as social suffering, enabling them to stake their historical claims and thereby restore their dignity.

But as long as women have to resort to "widowhood" to be able to make claims on a society that does not recognize the wounds it inflicts on the dream of full citizenship for women will remain unattainable. The retreat of women into nonthreatening, traditional roles may offer benefits, but they come at a price.

# C. Protecting Cultures

DANIEL GOLEMAN

*Humans have developed thousands of distinctive cultures, but widespread social change and technology threaten to destroy many of them. Anthropologists, who specialize in the study of culture, have become concerned about this threat and have begun to take an activist stand to protect cultures. This reading describes the efforts of the American Anthropological Association and raises the issues of cultural preservation and change.*

At the stroke of midnight on Nov. 10, 1983, the creation of a new national park in Sri Lanka made cultural orphans of the Wanniya-laeto, the last remnant of a people who appear to have lived on the island for 28,000 years. The final fringe of the forests in which they had been hunters and gatherers was put off limits for all hunting and gathering of food. A Wanniya-laeto who tried to stick to the old ways would be arrested as a poacher.

Since then, the Wanniya-laeto, split into three groups, have been struggling to preserve their culture. And earlier this year the American Anthropological Association, the discipline's largest and most prestigious professional group, took a small step to aid the Wanniya-laeto, but a big step for anthropology. It sent a letter to the Prime Minister of Sri Lanka, Sirimavo Bandaranaike, to protest the treatment of the Wanniya-laeto people, and to ask that they be allowed to live once again on park lands or have access to them.

That was the first formal action by a Committee for Human Rights established by the association last October in a step designed to move anthropology as a profession to an activist stance taken only erratically in the past, and usually by individual anthropologists. The letter marked the first time the anthropological association itself has actively intervened in a dispute, although it has taken political positions in the past. The association includes both cultural anthropologists, who study cultural groups of people, and physical anthropologists, who study the physical characteristics of humans and their ancestors.

"The mandate of the rights committee is broad," said its chairman, Dr. Tom Greaves, an anthropologist at

*Reprinted from Daniel Goleman, "Anthropology Group Takes Activist Stand to Protect Cultures," THE NEW YORK TIMES, March 10, 1996, P. C 1, 4. Reprinted with permission of the NY Times Company.*

Bucknell University. "While our interventions frequently relfect our concern for the welfare of the isolated peoples who have so often hosted our resarch," Dr. Graves said, "our concern is with any group of persons where assaults on their cultural ways have put them in danger."

In addition to the plight of the dispossessed Wanniya-laeto, who can no longer continue their traditional ways as forest-dwellers, the association has now taken up the causes of other cultures as well, lodging complaints with governments and other official groups, like the World Bank. It has protested the mistreatment and displacement of Maya Indians by the Guatemalan Army, the execution of leaders of the Ogoni tribe by the Nigerian Government and the seizing of the lands of the Uanomami Indians in Brazil and Venezuela by gold miners.

One reason for the new activism is concern over the disappearance of cultures, a problem that appears to have become more serious in the last century or two.

While no one can say with exact certainty at what rate cultures are becoming extinct worldwide, Dr. Patrick Morris, an anthropologist at the University of Washington, said, "At least a third of the world's inventory of human cultures have disappeared completely since 1500—their languages, their traditions and ways of life, their world view and very identity."

The peoples most at risk are those who are indigenous, the original inhabitants of a land. Often in the areas where they live, biological diversity, the wide range of plant and animal species, is threatened as well.

Dr. David Maybury-Lewis, an anthropologist at Harvard University, said: "The roughly 5 percent of the world population who are Indigenous people are being seriously threatened worldwide. Cultural diversity is an important world resource, as essential to the resilience of the human race in the long run as is biological diversity."

The move to activism by the anthropologists has ignited a debate within the field, with some protesting that such advocacy blurs the discipline's objectivity, or can be perceived as doing so. Others argue that anthropologists have both a moral and professional obligation to protect the people who make the discipline possible by opening their way of life to study.

"When you live for months in a community," said Dr. Greaves, "when the success of your field work depends on the generosity and patience of people who probably didn't invite you but who took you in anyway, a bond of friendship and mutual obligation results. When they encounter abuse, we feel a need to act."

Other anthropologists worry that mixing moral or political concerns with their professional work will dilute their ability to do good science. Dr. Roy D'Andrade, an anthropologist at the University of California at San Diego, said in a letter to The Anthropology Newsletter that "our moral models about the anthropologist's responsibilities should be kept separate from our models about the world," adding, "otherwise the result will be very bad science and very confused morality."

On a more practical level, some anthropologists have expressed concern that activism will displease some governments and lead the m to deny anthropologists access to the people they wish to study—or take even more severe steps. "Anthropologists have given their lives in Ethiopia, Guatemala and South Africa," Dr. Morris said, "to protect people they worked with."

A politically active approach can backfire. In 1991, a Canadian judge ruled against a land claim by the Gitskan and Wet'suwet'en tribes, supported by testimony by three anthropologists. The judge rejected the anthropologists' testimony, saying they were playing a partisan role rather than giving a reliable, impartial presentation of data.

In disregarding the anthropologists' testimony, the judge cited an article of the Principles of Professional Responsibility of the anthropological association, part of which reads: "In research, an anthropologist's paramount responsibility is to those he studies. When there is a conflict of interest, these individuals must come first."

That principle, which was formalized in 1968, has led to what some anthropologists say amounts to a generational schism within the profession. Many anthropologists trained in the 1970s and 1980s were taught that their profession demanded an activist stand.

Younger anthropologists are often in the lead in speaking up for threatened peoples. The case of the Wanniya-laeto people in Sri Lanka, for example, is being championed by Wiveca Stegeborn, a graduate student at Syracuse University.

The Wanniya-laeto, known more widely as the Veddahs, have inhabited Sri Lanka for more than 28,000 years, according to archeological evidence. They now number just over 2,000 people.

"Originally, they were all over the Island, until the Sinhalese came 2,500 years ago," Ms. Stegeborn said. "Over the centuries, they've gradually retreated and retreated, until now they have no place to go except this last patch of jungle that's now been taken away from them in the name of making it a game park."

Ms. Stegeborn added: "In the years since they were forced from the jungle, they've been split up into several farflung villages, where it's harder and harder to follow their traditional ways. They've always lived off the jungle; now they end up on welfare or do the most mental labor."

Because of Ms. Stegeborn's efforts, the cause of the Winniya-laeto was the first to be backed officially by the new rights committee. The association's letter objecting to the resettlement of the Wanniya-laeto contends that the action violated international law, and it requested that the Sri Lankan Government take remedial action.

"I absolutely believe anthropologists have to take a stand on these disappearing peoples," Ms. Stegeborn said, "and do something about saving what's left. Otherwise, it's like a surgeon simply watching a patient die and making clinical observations about the fading pulse without trying to save him."

# Resource Page

## A. THE LIMITS TO CULTURAL DIVERSITY

### Study Questions

• How diverse are the many cultures of humankind?
• What does the author mean by "an excess of cultural identity"?
• What is the difference between culture and civilization, and why is the difference important?
• How does the author propose to solve the problem of excessive cultural identity?

### Key Concepts

civil society
civilization
cultural diversity
cultural identity

### Additional Resources

• Lawrence E. Harrison. *Who Prospers? How Cultural Values Shape Economic and Political Success.* New York: Basic Books, 1992. Why culture makes a differenc
• James Davison Hunter. *Culture Wars: The Struggle to Define America.* New York: BasicBooks, 1991. A good review of the multiculturalism debate.
•George Spindler, Henry T. Trueba and Melvin D. Williams. *The American Cultural Dialogue and Its Transmission.* Bristol, PA: Falmer Press, 1990. An excellent review of America's multiculturism debate.

## B. WIDOWHOOD IN SOUTH AFRICA

### Study Questions

• What are some aspects of the "widowhood" status in South African society?
• When do funerals move from occassions of private mourning to public and political events?
• How does political widowhood lead to role strain?
• How does the status of "widowhood" contribute to the social structure of South African society?

### Key Concepts

liminal phase
political widowhood
mourning ritual

### Additional Resources

• Erving Goffman. *Stigma: Notes on the Management of Spoiled Identity.* Englewood Cliffs, NJ: Prentice-Hall, 1963. An excellent treatment of status.
• Paul Rosenblatt. *Grief and Mourning in Cross-Cultural Perspective.* New Haven, CN: HRAG Press, 1976. A basic treatment of death in many cultures.

## C. PROTECTING CULTURES

### Study Questions

• Who is American Anthropolgy Association and what are some of the cultures they want to protect?
• What particular problems do these centuries-old indigenous cultures currently face?
• How do the Maya Indians and Ogmi tribe illustrate the evolution of socieites as described on pp. 33-37 of the text?
• Should the U.S. help protect ancient cultures?

### Key Concepts

cultural advocacy
cultural anthropology
cultural diversity

### Additional Resources

• Ignacio Bizarro-Ujpan. *Son of Tecun Uman: A Maya Indian Tells His Life Story.* Tucson, AR: University of Arizona Press, 1981. A good history of Mayan life.
• Carol Ember and Melvin Ember. *Anthropology: A Brief Introduction*, 2nd Edition. Englewood Cliffs, NJ, Prentice-Hall, 1995. An excellent introduction to anthropology.
• Marvin Harris. *Our Kind.* New York: HarperCollins, 1990. This collection of essays describes social evolution
• Gene Lisitsky. *Four Ways of Being Human.* New York: Viking Press, 1955. A classic.

# A. Early Childhood Socialization in Hispanic Families

LUIS H. ZAYAS AND FABIANA SOLARI

*While socialization occurs among every human group, different ethnic cultures teach their children different ideas and values. In the U.S., most studies have focused on socialization among the major cultural group; only recently has research begun to study more fully distinctive ethnic patterns of socialization. This reading focuses on the special situations that occur in Hispanic families and show Show they differ from other cultural groups.*

Although there have been some empirical and theoretical advances made in our understanding of minority child socialization, most of our existing knowledge comes from studies of middle-class Euro-American families. This means that our assumptions about normative child rearing behaviors and beliefs and child competencies rest upon a Euro-American set of values. The unfortunate implication is that child socialization processes that differ from these value-laded assumptions are deviant.

A small but growing body of research has confirmed what has been intuitively apprehended that in socializing their children, parents from ethnic and racial minorities use distinct beliefs and behaviors determined largely by their cultural and socioeconomic situation and is often intended to prepare children for the society they will encounter, a society in which the minority child, as one expert stated, "finds out immediately ... that the color of his skin or the background of his parents rather than his wish and will to learn are the factors that decide his worth."

The emerging literature suggests that socialization in minority families if often intended to prepare children for the society they will encounter, a society in which the minority child, as Erikson states, "finds out immediately...that the color of his skin or the background of his parents rather than his wish and will to learn are the factors that decide his worth. In this article, we bring together some recent findings regarding the socialization of young children in Hispanic families."

Across cultures, a person's early development usually takes place within the milieu of a family. Parents'

*Excerpted from Luis H. Zayas and Fabiana Solari, "Early Childhood Socialization in Hispanic Families: Context, Culture, and Practice Implications," PROFESSIONAL PSYCHOLOGY, RESEARCH, AND PRACTICE, Vol. 25, No. 1, 1994, pp. 200-205.*

interactions with children typically include a hierarchy of priorities, such as ensuring their children's physical health, survival, and self-maintenance as the child grows while fostering capacities that maximize cultural values. With their preschool children, parents often focus on regulating the children's affective states by directly dealing with children's emotional expressions and monitoring the children's moment-to-moment activities and providing feedback. Effective psychosocial functioning emerges from these interactions and endures well beyond the time children are physically dependent on their parents.

One window into the socialization process is afforded by the child rearing values of the parents' ethnocultural reference group. Minority group parents have culturally determined developmental goals for their children and, therefore, their reactions, perceptions, and behaviors will differ from majority group parents. Among Hispanic and other minority families of low socioeconomic status, for instance, the need for adequate child care may require the mobilization of the extended family. Thus, a child's attachment to several significant adult relatives may be an important source of socialization despite the presence of the parents as the primary caregivers.

The cumulative effects of socioeconomic disadvantage and negative stereotyping felt by racial and ethnic minority families leads them to develop adaptive strategies based on their beliefs about what it means to be a member of an ethnic or racial minority group. Adaptive strategies arise from the need to survive and to maintain continuity from one generation to the next. Families then formulate socialization goals to teach their children the strategies necessary for survival.

One example of an adaptive strategy and socialization goal that Hispanic families have drawn from their culture and experience is the emphasis on family solidarity and the individual's sense of obligation to the family. This strategy helps protect the family's continuity and preserve its culture. In low-income Hispanic families, parents and the extended family serve as the primary mentors for transmitting important values of the culture. The socialization goal that emerges is to have children accept that family is to be the central focus of their lives. A child rearing practice that incorporates these goals is the insistence on children's conformity to parental and extended-family authority, which often extends to conformity to the authority of other adults as well. Aside from reflecting the esteem given to parents and the importance of family relatedness, this socialization practice helps identify development, which is intimately tied to the family in Hispanic cultures.

As children age and develop, parents' supervision of and interaction with their children changes. Yet, most parents maintain a consistent rationale and approach to socialization—a rhyme and reason—that is influenced by ethnic, racial, and cultural beliefs and values. For minority parents, this means engaging in interaction with children not only to help them develop the skills for such adult roles as wage-earning and parenthood, but also to help socialize them so they will be able to negotiate a dominant society that has different cultural beliefs and that often judges people by the color of their skin or their ethnic background.

In most Hispanic families, parents socialize children to behave in ways important to the family's culture, whether or not it is in accordance with the norms of the dominant culture. One study looked at valued school behaviors promoted by low-income Puerto Rican mothers with children in a Headstart program, in comparison with Anglo-American teachers' expectations of these children. Puerto Rican mothers prefer obedience, rule following and conformity in the classroom, while Anglo-American teachers and parents prefer independence, verbal expressiveness, and self-directed activities. Mothers operated from a set of values more characteristic of traditional Puerto Rican beliefs.

Another recent study of parents' beliefs illustrates the differences that can exist between parental and school expectations. Immigrant parents from Cambodia, Mexico, the Philippines, and Vietnam and native-born Anglo-Americans and Mexican Americans, whose children were in kindergarten through first grade, were asked questions about their child rearing beliefs and expectations for children's behavior in school and their thoughts on what characterized an intelligent child. Immigrant parents rated conforming to external standards as being more important to instill in their children than developing autonomous behaviors. In contrast, American-born parents favored developing autonomy over conformity. Parents from all groups except Anglo-Americans indicated that noncognitive characteristics (i.e., motivation, social skills, and practical school skills) were as important as or more important than cognitive characteristics (such as problem-solving skills and verbal and creative ability).

Overall, the emerging literature on early childhood socialization in Hispanic families points to some specific child rearing values and practices that are influenced by the families' culture and contexts. Mexican-American, Puerto Rican, and other Hispanic parents appear to prefer behaviors in children that encourage family closeness, parental authority, and interpersonal relatedness. Continued research is needed to expand our understanding of the impact of culture and context on child socialization in Hispanic families.

# B. It's Time To Rethink Nature and Nurture

GEOFFREY COWLEY

*Despite decades of debate, social scientists have still not agreed upon the relative impact of nature and nurture in shaping human behavior. Recently, many writers have reasserted the key role of biological factors in explaining human differences, but others have continued to argue that culture creates all that we are. This reading reviews research on the nature versus nurture debate and recognizes the key role of each in shaping humans' diverse behaviors.*

Everyday, science seems to chip away at our autonomy. When researchers aren't uncovering physical differences in the way men and women use their brains, they're asserting genetic influences on intelligence, sexual orientation, obesity or alcoholism. Or they're suggesting that the level of some brain chemical affects one's chances of committing violent crimes. Each new finding leaves the impression that nature is winning out over nurture—that biology is destiny and free will an illusion. But the nature-nurture dichotomy is itself an illusion. As many scholars are now realizing, everything we associate with "nurture" is at some level a product of our biology—and every aspect of our biology, from brain development to food preference, has been shaped by an environment. Asking whether nature or nurture is more important is like asking whether length or width is a better gauge of size.

Darwin recognized more than 100 years ago that Homo sapiens evolved by the same process as every other species on earth. And philosophers such as William James were eager to apply Darwin's insights to human psychology. But during the first part of this century, the rise of "social Darwinism" (a non-Darwinian, sink-or-swim political philosophy) and later Nazi eugenics spawned a deep suspicion of biologically inspired social science. By 1954, anthropologist Ashley Montagu was declaring that mankind has "no instincts because everything he is and has become he has learned, acquired, from his culture."

The distinction between innate and acquired seems razor sharp, until you try slicing life with it. Consider the development of the brain. While gestating in the womb, a child develops some 50 trillion neurons. But those cells

become functional only as they respond to outside stimuli. During the first year of life, the most frequently stimulated neurons form elaborate networks for processing information, while the others wither and die. You could say that our brains determine the structure of our experiences—or that experience determines the structure of our brains.

Social behavior follows the same principle. From the old nature-versus-nurture perspective, a tendency that isn't uniformly expressed in every part of the world must be "cultural" rather than "natural." But there is no reason to assume that a universal impulse would always find the same expression. As the evolutionists John Tooby and Leda Cosmides have observed, biology can't dictate what language a child will speak, what games she'll play, what rites she'll observe or what she'll feel guilty or jealous about. But it virtually guarantees that she'll do all of those things, whether she grows up in New Jersey or New Guinea.

Biology, in short, doesn't determine exactly what we'll do in life. It determines how different environments will affect us. And our biology is itself a record of the environments our ancestors encountered. Consider the sexes' different perceptual styles. Men tend to excel at spatial reasoning, women at spoting stationary objects and remembering their locations. Such discrepancies may have a biological basis, but researchers have traced the biology back to specific environmental pressures. Archeological findings suggest that men hunted, and women foraged, throughout vast stretches of evolutionary time. And psychologists Irwin Silverman and Marion Eals have noted that "tracking and killing animals entail different kinds of spatial problems than does foraging for edible plants."

Unfortunately, a trait shaped by one environment can become deadly in another. Craving fat, and storing it efficiently, would promote survival in a setting where food sources were scarce and unpredictable. But the same

*Reprinted from Geoffrey Cowley, "It's Time to Rethink Nature and Nurture," NEWSWEEK, March 27, 1995, pp. 52-53. Reprinted by permission of NEWSWEEK.*

tendencies cause mass heart failure when expressed in a fast-food paradise. Alcoholism wasn't even possible in the environments where humankind evolved, yet it has plagued the world since the advent of brewer's yeast. In a preagricultural setting, the evolutionists Randolph Nesse and George Williams speculate in their new book, "Why We Get Sick," the biological traits that now foster compulsive drinking might have had "positive effects—for instance, a tendency to [pursue] sources of reward despite difficulties."

Violent crime, like overeating and drunkenness, has clear biological roots, but that doesn't mean it's inherent in anyone's nature. Males come outfitted for aggression in many sexually reproducing species, and some human males seem constitutionally more volatile than others. Since the 1970s, numerous studies have linked criminal violence to low levels of the brain chemical serotonin. That association has led some experts, including former National Institute of Mental Health director Frederick Goodwin, to view criminality as a medical disorder that might be predicted through blood testing and prevented through chemical treatment. But the biology of crime isn't that simple. As social critic Robert Wright noted in a recent New Yorker article, low serotonin may leave people more prone to violence—but poor social conditions seem to lower serotonin levels. Perhaps the best way to counter the biological causes of urban crime, he concludes, is to create better schools and higher paying jobs—to turn the inner cities into "places where young men have nonviolent routes to social status."

The talk of a pharmaceutical war on crime can only feed the suspicions of liberals like Harvard geneticist Richard Lewontin, who warned in 1984 that "if human social organization ... is a direct consequence of our biologies, then, except for some gigantic program of genetic engineering, no practice can make a significant alternation of social structure." But there is nothing inherently determinist about a biological perspective—and nothing to be gained by pretending that we live outside of nature.

Biology shapes our impulses and aptitudes, but it doesn't act alone. There is always a context, and always room for resistance. "It's biologically implausible to have a gene for something like crime," Sir Michael Rutter, the British child psychiatrist, observed recently. "It's like saying there's a gene for Roman Catholicism." When that precise a gene is found, we'll have to give up on free will. For now, its status seems safe.

# C. "Edutaining" Children

MILLIE R. CREIGHTON

*Socialization, the complex process whereby persons learn the values and roles of their culture, takes place throughout childhood. In today's consumer-oriented societies, this process includes learning about buying goods and about shopping malls. This reading describes how Japanese children are taught their society's values in shopping centers, which offer activities that both entertain and educate children. This "edutaining" helps children become full participants in Japan's industrial and consumer economy.*

A common Japanese expression asserts, "Ko wa takara," (children as treasures). In present day Japan, the perception of children as treasures often implies indulging them with unprecedented consumer offerings. A spokesperson for a company that designs child-oriented shopping theme parks told me in a 1991 interview that the children's market was the predicted preeminent arena of Japanese consumerism for the decade of the 1990s. What was perhaps most significant about this statement is that in 1990 Japan marked a new all-time record low birthrate for the eleventh year in a row.

Far from foretelling the doom of children's sales, Japan's declining birthrate has propelled goods and services directed at children to new extremes. Children themselves also have more money to spend. As the actual birthrate declined, Japan witnesses the birth of the "five pocket child," meaning that with so few children, each child now receives larger fists of money from several indulging sources, and hence metaphorically needs one pocket each for money received from parents, grandparents, aunts and uncles, neighboring households, and others.

This article reports on the construction of shopping worlds for parents and children in Japan. It presumes that not only consumer goods, but promotional catalogues and even the physical space of store layouts constitute cultural objects. These establish a physical reality heavily imbued with symbolic meaning and thus "create a setting for behavior" that compels people toward certain forms of action. To address these issues, I utilize the concept of edutainment. Edutainment is the fusion of education and entertainment offerings, particularly popular or mass culture entertainments that take on educating functions or

*Excerpted from Millie R. Creighton, "'Edutaining' Children: Consumer and Gender Socialization in Japanese Marketing,"* ETHNOLOGY, Winter, 1994, pp. 35 ff.

invoke a pretense of having such functions. Invoking education in Japan serves to legitimize many hobbies or leisure activities that might otherwise be construed as overly indulgent fun.

Beginning in the 1980s, then escalating rapidly from 1990, the upsurge in children's marketing resulted in the appearance of shopping theme parks for children, which many observers feel now rival the entertainment atmosphere of Tokyo Disneyland. In addition to their amusement orientation, these specialty shopping parks echo the educational and cultural development themes, while again providing kids' clubs where members actually meet and interact.

From 1990, shopping theme parks designed as play floors for children were open one after another. Seibu transformed the entire seventh floor of its main store into a kids farm. Tokyo Sesame Place, fashioned after Sesame Place built a decade earlier in the U.S., opened in 1990.

When Seibu opened kids farm, iIt amalgamated all previous store sections dealing with child-related goods or services, and also amalgamated its former Baby Circle, Young Tyke's Circle, and other children's clubs into a new "escalator" club series called the kids farm club. Seibu added several highly sophisticated children's boutiques, such as Ralph Lauren, Christian Dior, and Tartine et Chocalat, a Paris designer line for children, all aimed at fashion conscious "campus-minded mamas."

Kids farm combines new amusement services, such as emloyees dressed as clowns to entertain children or a mountain-climbing play area, with new learning opportunities. At a special area of kids farm, called "First Science Corner," specialist employees conduct science experiments with children. Kids farm also offers English conversation lessons specifically for children.

As it name suggests, Dr. Kids Town has been

designed as a miniature town for children, and is said to be a representation of a small American rural town. The young female staff at Dr. Kids Town socialize with the children, contributing to an atmosphere reminiscent of a preschool or elementary school. Visitors are allowed to play freely throughout town. Children can be seen riding tricycles or skate boarding (using store merchandise) through the brick streets, or playing in the sponge pool while adults rest on town benches. Children climb the fire engine, enter the log homes, and the five hourses of the foreign character children. Within these housesthey can play with their foreign playmates' toys, or rest in their beds.

The designers of Dr. Kids Town not only created a theme park for children, but constructed an educational philosophy to go along with it. The educational philosophy of Dr. Kids Town can be found on placards located on the shop floor, and also in the user's guide to Dr. Kids Town for parents, called "For Your Future Growth: Dr. Kids." A Dr. Kids spokesperson explained that the theme park has a social message. It is that all Japanese must start thinking about developing children as Japan's resources for the 21st century, that parents are really only concerned with their own child or children, hoping they get into good universities and so on. But, she continued, not all children will get into prestigious universities, and Japan as a society could not exist in the future if this were possible, since the society needs all kinds of people, with different abilities, doing different things.

The theme park shopping centers for children presented here show how far retailers' inclination to provide "princess and lord service" to Japan's youngest consumer market extends. The theme parks themselves, the special learning corners found within them, the accredited classes offered, the special entertainments, and even the merchandise for sale, all promise to educate the young. Often children do learn about science, math, language, etc. while their parents learn ways to cope with Japan's educational challenge. However, perhaps more than anything else, the edutainment offerings of the theme parks are educating children about their future roles, sometimes indirectly through sex-typed characters, and socializing them into expected patterns of consumer activity.

I have argued that stores constitute institutions of informal education. Stores, embedded in a culture, reflecting and shaping social trends within that culture, need to be considered sites of socialization, and of pedagogy. One

way in which Japanese stores function as institutions of informal learning is through their immense entertainment offerings, which frequently also invoke appeals to education. Given the relevant overlap of entertainment and education, I have suggested the term, "edutainment" as a tool for discussing the fusion and interplay of these two processes.

The large Japanese retailing complexes described here fulfill a socialization function through edutainment in three ways. The first involves direct messages about education. Store promotions and special events reflect the strong ideological value exalting education in Japan, as well as the pragmatic concerns surrounding education as the means to a desired life style.

Like other behaviors, consumerism involves learned, patterned actions. A second way in which store edutainment functions as a socializing agent is through the inculcation of appropriate consumer behavior. While socializing children into culturally defined appropriate age and gender consumer behavior, store discourse, communicated through the cultural objects of catalogues, advertisements, and the physical space of store layouts, constructs a role for modern consumerism consistent with prevailing cultural values. Consumerism is presented not so much as a way of finding oneself but as a means of linking selves to others.

The third way store edutainment functions as a socializing agent, is by prompting people more generally toward socially accepted values and behaviors. Stores do this by perpetuating themes common in Japanese society, providing images which define various social roles and by replicating gender expects. The images of children presented by the stores serve to mirror desired characteristics for Japanese children.

# Resource Page

## A. EARLY CHILDHOOD SOCIALIZATION IN HIS PANIC FAMILIES

### Study Questions

• How do parents shape socialization to prepare a member of a minority group for future interaction in society?
• What is meant by "adaptive strategies" and why are they important to racial and ethnic minority groups?
• What are some of the specific adaptation strategies of Hispanic groups?

### Key Concepts

adaptive strategies
ethnocultural reference group
socialization goals

### Additional Resources

• Federick Elkin and Gerald Handel. *The Child and Society.* 4th ed. New York: Random House, 1984. This classic text explores the impact of ethnicity and on childhood.
• Melvin Konner. *Childhood: A Multicultural View.* Boston: Little, Brown, 1991. This text provides a clear but technical view of childhood socialization.
• Clifton L. Taulbert. *Once Upon a Time When We Were Colored.* Tulsa, OK: Council Oaks Books, 1989. This beautiful book, recently made into a film, describes life in the deep South during segregation.

## B. IT'S TIME TO RETHINK NATURE AND NURTURE

### Study Questions

• What is the issue raised in the nature/nurture debate?
• Why does the author feel nature and nurture are inseparable?
• How can the interaction of nature and nurture explain cultural differences?

### Key Concepts

environment
free will
innate characteristics

### Additional Resources

• Ruth Hubbard and Elijah Wald. *Exploding The Gene Myth.* Boston: Beacon Press, 1993. A disturbing critique of genetic research and manipulation.
• Richard Herrnstein and Charles Murray. *The Bell Curve* New York: Free Press, 1994. A controversial book.
• Russ Rymer. *Genie: A Scientific Tragedy.* New York: HarperCollins Publishers, 1993. An excellent account of a severely isolated child and the efforts to help her.

## C. 'EDUTAINING' CHILDREN

### Study Questions

• What does the article's author mean by "edutaining"?
• What agencies of socialization are involved in providing instruction to children in Japanese shopping malls?
• What socialization practices in U.S. society are similar to those of Japan?
• What does "edutaining" tell us about global patterns of socialization?

### Key Concepts

construction of shopping worlds
edutaining
shopping themeparks

### Additional Resources

• William Goodsen. *Day Care in Three Societies.* New Haven, CN: Yale University Press, 1991. This study compares the uses of daycare in three cultures.
• Andrew B. Schmookler. *The Illusion of Choice: How the Market Economy Shapes Our Destiny.* Albany, NY: State University of New York Press, 1993. A good analysis of the role consumerism in modern culture.
• Ken Schoolland. *Shogun's Ghost: The Dark Side of Japanese Eeucation.* Westport, CN: Bergin & Garvey, 1990. This book is a look at aspects of education in Japan.

# A. Japanese and American Worker Interaction

LAURA MILLER

*Sociologists have discovered that social interaction is a subtle and complicated process that involves cultures. One approach to this subject in the text is ethnomethodology, which is an approach for discovering hidden meanings in social interaction. This reading is a good example of the ethnomethodological approach. The author used videotapes and transcripts to analyze persons from two different cultures to discover hidden patterns of social interaction.*

Articles and books that discuss Japanese and American intercultural communication use a variety of sources as a basis for their characterizations but rarely that of actual encounters themselves. The aim of this article is to illustrate how examination of natural interactions may reveal further information about communication between co-workers from different cultural backgrounds. As an alternative to the "cultures collide" perspective, this approach is based on a situational and interactive model of intercultural and interethnic communication where the actual interaction is the focus of microanalysis.

To collect data on what actually happens between Japanese and American co-workers, I conducted ethnographic observation at three firms in Tokyo that employed both Japanese and American workers. Analyses are based on observations, interviews and transcriptions of talk from naturally occurring conversations, which were audiotaped and videotaped. Two of the firms were advertising agencies, and one was a shipping company. All of the Americans had worked with their Japanese colleagues for at least a year. They all spoke Japanese with various degrees of proficiency.

How do workers in these firms create a sense of themselves as fellow employees and colleagues rather than as either Japanese or American? I believe that these Japanese and American co-workers rely on both customary interactive methods as well as new ways of exhibiting a sense of identification with their work groups. A few of the techniques I have identified include exchange of complaints about both personal and job-related topics, joking and teasing between co-workers, conversations in a form of mixed English and Japanese, talk that has an echoing effect,

* Excerpted from Laura Miller, "Two Aspects of Japanese and American Co-Worker Interaction: Giving Instructions and Creating Rapport." JOURNAL OF APPLIED BEHAVIORAL SCIENCE, June, 1995, pp. 141-161.

appropriate listening behavior, and use of shared office space. The findings indicate that even in such bicultural settings demonstrating a sense of group identity is an important and valued aspect of workplace behavior.

One of the most common ways in which workers demonstrated group cohesion was through the introduction of joking and teasing into a conversation. By finding something they can agree on as humorous, they exhibit a sense of co-membership and alignment. Joining in with another's complaining provides an additional way to display solidarity. Generally, Japanese co-workers feel comfortable complaining about their families, health, jobs, children's school, and housing to each other and expect an empathetic listener to sympathize with or upgrade the complaints. Although complaining to outsiders is not always appropriate, cooperative complaining among group members is an important aspect of sharing and empathizing.

Other aspects of talk that exhibit the existence of a group mentality among Japanese and American co-workers are exchanging praise and something I have termed "echoing talk." Co-workers often comment on each other's personality, sociability, skills and good nature. Compliments on appearance, however, are not very common. Echoing talk is a phenomena in which two or three co-workers repeat a work or phrase in succession. This echoing talk demonstrates a group orientation and a type of collaboration in thinking as though each is achieving the same thought.

Most of the workers I observed did not participate in group-bonding activities championed by popular writers such as playing golf together, exchanging gifts, eating and drinking out together and masking supposedly individualistic tendencies. Nevertheless, they all exhibited evidence of group identity and rapport. Although they often experienced other interactional problems, they nevertheless exhibited a strong sense of cohesion and togetherness. This demonstrates that even in bicultural situations, the construction and display of a group identity is an important aspect of workplace behavior.

The videotapes collected in Tokyo provide some of the first empirical documentation of what, in fact, actually happens in these intercultural workplace interactions. They enable analyses that do not always confirm stereotyped and widespread characterizations of Japanese and American communication. One, we can teach ourselves and others to become something like "mini-ethnographers" in any type of multicultural setting. We can ask what sort of situation it is, what cultural meanings and expectations attach to it, and what roles and behaviors are consequently considered appropriate. We must also start with our own cultural presuppositions and make these explicit first. In the same way that American cultural behavior is situationally dependent and not easily boiled down to a menu of traits— the same silence appropriate to a funeral may indicate interactional difficult during an interview-the behavior of those from other cultural backgrounds is equally complex and situation-dependent.

Second, we can recognize that no matter how much training and preparation we do, no matter how well we speak the language and understand the culture, there will invariably be occasions of misunderstanding and misinterpretation. The important point to keep in mind is that these misunderstandings can sneak up on us, that they often occur without our even knowing it. Given the insidious nature of these pragmatic misunderstandings, we need to be alert to those times when we find ourselves making negative character and/or ethnic assessments and evaluations (such as "he's too direct" or "she's too evasive") because these are often a clue to underlying difference. It is at these junctures that we should step back and ask, " What assumptions and expectations are these assessments based on, and what cultural differences may be in operation here and now?"

Lastly, despite the various problems that can arise in any multicultural setting, it is not imperative to view every interaction as a raging battlefield of contrasting values and beliefs. In many cases, workers are able to overcome differences and misunderstandings to forge productive cohesion. So as we stand alert to the potential for misunderstanding, let us also hold the everyday talk through which people negotiate their lives in higher esteem. Rather than denigrate behavior such as joking, complaining, and other types of small talk as frivolous, we should recognize their role in helping to create a valuable sense of group solidarity and identity.

# B. The Court and the Kola Nut

SUSAN DRUCKER-BROWN

*One significant aspect of social interaction in everyday life is the performance of interaction rituals. The text points out that the purpose of these rituals is to show reverence to others, which allows social interaction to proceed. This reading analyzes an important interaction ritual found in Northern Ghana, which is the gift of kola nuts. The purpose of this ritual is to maintain a sense of sociability and patterns of Mamprusi society.*

In all of the centralized and centralizing polities of northern Ghana, the kola nut is an ubiquitous companion of chiefship. A Mamprusi chief distributes kola to his people and an offering of kola is placed daily in the shrine which houses the king's ancestors. A stranger, taken to see a chief, always carries a literal or metaphorical gift of kola. For Mamprusi people, a presentation of kola is the crucial act which establishes legitimate marriage, and the marriage kola should be transferred through a chief. Kola is formally distributed at many other events; at funerals and naming ceremonies, at communal work parties, when rights to land are requested and, again, when they are transferred. Kola nuts are exchanged informally between friends, and individuals buy kola for their own private consumption. It is given as alms to mallams, lepers or the blind. Placed at crossroads, or the entrance to anthills, it serves to elicit prayers on behalf of the donor. The contexts in which kola is used thus vary from the individual and private to the most public and collective.

Kola is the nut of the tree cola nitida which grows in the East African rainforest. Kola is not indigenous to the savannah region in which the Mamprusi live and the kola nut is imported. Kola is a stimulant and is addictive, but it is very bitter. Children normally do not chew it, but young girls who sell kola or young boys who have started farming may have become accustomed to the taste by the age of 10 or 11. Kola symbolizes for Mamprusi that solidarity and "unencumbered sociability" which they desire but mistrust.

The association of kola with 'love' and the importance of the collective consumption of kola is illustrated in the following description of how kola should be distributed to a group of farmers.

*Excerpted from Susan Drucker-Brown, "The Court and the Kola Nut: Wooing and Witnessing in Northern Ghana." JOURNAL OF THE ROYAL INSTITUTE OF ANTHROPOLOGY, January, 1995, pp. 129-143.*

If you summon people...you should give them kola to show that when you call them together to tell them something, and you have followed ancestral practice in the activity of the meeting, the kola should be broken to let the group feel that they are part of a group and to feel their love for one another. Many people will not be happy if you gather them and don't give kola to show your love for the group and (enable them to show) their love for one another.

In the case of a communal farming party, those who receive kola may reasonably expect the farmer who distributes it to reciprocate their efforts on this farm, by farming with them on their farms in the future. This reciprocity is not rigidly defined or enforced: it is part on an on-going relationship among neighbors; part of an exchange in which measurements are flexible and the value of gifts is counter against what the giver can afford. Kola is typically used to initiate or continue such on-going relationships.

The use of kola to produce witnesses of an event is most clearly evident in the use of kola at marriage. In the giving of marriage kola the following rules are observed:

1)      The kola must be received by the head of the bride's 'gate (a patri-lineage segment).
However, no man may receive the pardon kola for his own daughter and if a woman is the daughter of a gate-head, the next most senior man of his generation, or the most senior member of the nest generation, will receive the kola.

2)      All members of the senior generation of both the bride's parents' gates must receive some portion of the pardon kola even if it is only a fragment.

3)      Where the couple are from different villages two chiefs must receive the kola.

4)      Anyone who receives a portion of the marriage kola should chew some part of it immediately.

In case of divorce the kola and gift of money which constitute pardon kola are not refundable. By contrast, the return of other gifts made during courtship may be demanded. Here again, kola creates witnesses. Sending the message kola, unlike any of the arrangements which may have preceded the girl's disappearance, makes the king or chief and elders witnesses to the entire process from the announcement of the suitor's intent, through the reaction of the girl's parents and, finally, to the accord which is symbolized by acceptance of the pardon kola. The passage of kola through the court can be seen as a kind of registration of marriage, which is also an insurance in case such disputes arise. I have seen the king refuse to hear a divorce case in which he had not been part to the exchange of kola.

Mamprusi funerals are linked to marriage through the obligations of in-lawship, and one might say that these obligations are marked from the beginning of a marriage by the distribution of the marriage kola. Thus, a man is responsible for "performing the funeral" of members of the senior generations of his wife's parents. To "perform a funeral" means that a man should provide a sheep for sacrifice and come with his kin to dance, providing powder for the guns which they fire during funeral dances. Mamprusi funerals last for at least three days and nights during which time many people stay awake dancing, or observing, and elders guard the funeral guests and bereaved against attack by sorcerers and witches. The funeral-owners serve kola to the guests throughout this period. Kola is also given as payment to specialists: to those who dig the grave, to those who sew the shroud for burial, to the musicians and praise-singers, and to the Muslims who pray at the funeral's final phase. These prayers are accompanies by a public distribution of kola and often by a distribution of millet beer. The explicit meaning of the final gift of kola, here as in other cases, is that the kola is a thanks/greeting given by the hosts to those who have come to help. The thanks which the kola represents here, as in the greeting of a chief or the presentations of marriage kola, is a conditional thanks; a greeting which refers to both to past performance and to future obligation.

The kola which Mamprusi so value clearly serves to stimulate sociability and thus inherently appropriate to the wide variety of social situations in which it is used. In all these situations the giving of kola symbolizes ideals of amity and trust which should exist between donor and recipient and among those who chew kola together. The fear of poison in kola can be seen as a manifestation of the conflict which people feel between those ideals and the antagonisms they know to be present in the social contexts of the kola gift. In convening the court, in legitimizing marriage and in ending funerals, kola is consumed when amicable relations are desired and indeed asserted, but where conflict among those who chew kola together, may well arise.

This article has shown how kola both contributes to and symbolizes sociality in general and how, in addition, kola presentation draws from that generalized sociality a special role for the observer, whose ability to testify is linked to his or her part in the amicable and collective distribution of kola. Though kola is publicly distributed, it must be individually consumed. It is thus used to mark the individual observer who links the moment of distribution and consumption of kola to future events in which his or her testimony may be significant.

# C. White South Africans Learn Zulu and More

SARAH CROWE

*Language is a crucial aspect of social interaction and culture. Language contains a culture's meanings, values and ideas as well as important symbols, and learning the language of another culture introduces that culture's inner meanings. This reading provides an example of language's inner meanings. Here, in the new South Africa, white South Africans are learning Zulu and discovering many apsects of black-South African culture.*

For better and for worse, Dirk Hansen, a white South African, understands for the first time what the great majority of his black compatriots are saying behind his back.

Mr. Hansen, a Johannesburg banker, is one of a rapidly growing number of whites who are staking their claim to being true Africans by learning a black language.

Since South Africa's transformation to black majority rule, language schools have been swamped with requests from whites to learn Zulu and other African tongues among the country's 11 official languages.

In the past, apartheid dictated that the races live separate lives, which gave rise to a "them and us" culture between blacks and whites. Now they're officially allowed to get to know one another, and the creation of a new nation—often referred to as the "rainbow nation"—is under way.

For those whites who can now communicate in the vernacular, speaking Zulu has lifted a major barrier and opened a window on a once invisible world they passed by in their everyday lives. "Black people repond first with amazement then delight at this white face speaking their language," says Hansen, who has put in some 120 hours learning Zulu. "I've become one of their favorite people at the office. I used to think that blacks walked around with a huge chip on their shoulder, as if the white world owed them a living, but that opinion has waned a lot," he says. "Speaking Zulu has given me enormous respect for the black people and their culture."

For some of Hansen's classmates at Interman, a Johannesburg language school where the number of African teachers has increased threefold the past year because of the huge demand, it hasen't always been positive.

*Excerpted from Sarah Crowe, "White South Africans Learn Zulu and Much More." THE CHRISTIAN SCIENCE MONITOR, November 13, 1995, pp. 1, 13.*

'You can't believe how blacks talk about us all the time," says Joe McCrystal, a town planner. When you walk into a lift they natter on about you, thinking you don't understand a word they're saying. Sometimes you hear things you don't want to hear."

Much of the tension between the races in South Africa has often been put down to blacks and whites not knowing each other's culture and not being able to communicate properly. It's an explosive mix that many say can be tempered by whites learning a black language.

There was a time when for many whites, it would have been unthinkable to learn anything from blacks. They would be labeled a Kaffiboetie (derogatory term in Afrikaans meaning lover of blacks) or a communist.

Thembi Muyanga, a Zulu teacher at Interman, says she sees many of her students change from being closet racists to having a whole new vision of African culture.

'It's a really wonderful thing. It's part of the whole reconciliatory mood in the country to forget the past and go forward together," she says. "Whites start being able to see the light about us. There are so many things that they didn't understand. For instance, in Zulu culture you must not look at someone in the eye if you respect them, but whites think that is a sign that the person is not to be trusted. And we do not shake hands firmly or stand when the other person is sitting. It's important that these things are learned so we can understand each other better."

"Many whites see it as a form of social responsibility to make the effort to learn a black language and ease the transition to black rule," says Neil Bjorkman at Pill, a Johannesburg institution where the language demand has doubled in the past year.

This new rush to take up black languages is seen as a dramatic indication of a move away from Eurocentric behavior and a willingness among whites to accept their place in Africa.

Formerly, whites would have studied European languages such as French or German if they were going to learn a third language on top of English and Afrikaans. For 40 years those two "white" languages were the only official languages. Now, Afrikaans—a language similar to Dutch and the only European language to have originated in Africa—has the status of other African languages, and English is widely spoken in most cities as the language of business and politics.

Although it is only one of nine official African languages, Zulu is the linagua franca of the country and is understood by more than 70 percent of the people.

A cheapened form of colonial Zulu, Funigalo, or kitchen Zulu—essentially a language of basic comniands—was once used in South African mines and between whites and their black maids. But no self-respecting black person would answer to Funigalo today. So whites opt to learn Zulu, as it is a key to other languages in the Nguni group, such as Xhosa and Swazi.

"The reason for more and more whites learning Zulu and other black languages fits in with the ideas like the rainbow nation," says Dr. Gerard Schuring of the African language unit at the Human Sciences Research Council. "We are living in a multicultural and multilingual society and power has moved from whites to blacks, and blacks use African languages, so the whole political climate has become more conducive to this. There has been a definite shift, a greater admission and acceptance of the fact that we are in Africa."

"African languages have been boosted by the new Constitution, which demands that they be put on the same par as Afrikaans and English and promotes multilingualism," Dr. Schuring says.

He says that giving equal status to 11 official languages—English, Afrikaans, Zulu, SeTswana, Sesotho, Pedi, Shangaan, Venda, Xhosa, Ndebele, and Swazi—helps maintain peace and dignity and protects less popular languages.

In line with that thinking, several companies now include in their training schedules both African language courses and cross-cultural workshops, where blacks and whites come together to build bridges in the hope of determining a future for the nation that has less to do with its difficult past.

# Resource Page

## A. JAPANESE AND AMERICAN WORKER INTERACTION

### Study Questions

• What kind of intercultural interaction does this article examine?
• Why might Japanese and U.S. workers have intercultural communication problems?
• How did the author collect data for her study, and why was her approach unique?
• How did the Japanese and U.S. co-workers manage to establish rappor??

### Key Concepts

ethnography
multicultural setting
situated encounters

### Additional Resources

• Candace Clark and Howard Robboy. *Social Interaction: Readings in Sociology.* New York: St. Martin's Press, 1992. Many examples of social interaction.
• Harold Garfinkel. *Studies in Ethnomethology.* Cambridge, UK: Polity Press, 1967. This original book outlines ways to study everyday communication.
• Muriel Saville-Troike. *The Ethnography of Communication.* Baltimore: University Park Press, 1982. A basic text on language study.

## B. THE COURT AND THE KOLA NUT

### Study Questions

• What is the "kola nut" and how does it effect the mind?
• How is the kola nut used in Northern Ghanian rituals such as marriage?
• In what ways is the presentation of kola nuts an example of an interaction ritual?
• What interaction rituals in the U.S. are similar to the kola nut rituals described in the reading?

### Key Concepts

communal social life
interaction ritual
kola

### Additional Resources

• Irving Goffman. *Interaction Ritual.* Garden City, NY: Anchor Books, 1967. This classic work describes a variety of rituals that make up everyday life.
• Irving Goffman. *The Presentation of Self in Everyday Life.* New York: Doubleday, 1973. How presentation of ourselves is crucial to social life.
• Enid Schildkraut. *People of the Zongo: The Transformation of Ethnic Identities in Ghana.* New York, Cambridge University Press, 1978. Basic information about Ghana.

## C. WHITE SOUTH AFRICAN LEARN ZULU AND MORE

### Study Questions

• What has recently happened in South Africa that has caused whites learn Zulu??
• How has learning Zulu helped lift a major barrier and provided insight into a new world?
• How have black South Africans reacte to these efforts by whites to learn the language of blacks?

### Key Concepts

Funigalo
human communication
Zulu

### Additional Resources

• William B. Helmreich. *The Things They Say Behind Your Back: Stereotypes and the Myths Behind Them.* New Brunswick, NJ: Transaction Press, 1984. On stereotypes.
• Elinaor Ochs. *Culture and Language Development.* New York: Cambridge University Press, 1988. This text shows how language reflects aspects of culture.
• Nigel Worden. *The Making of Modern South Africa.* New York: Cambridge University Press, 1995. A basic history..

# A. Ultrasocial Darwinism

BRUCE BOWER

*An important characteristic of human life is living in groups. Humans cannot live, or reproduce themselves, on their own, but depend on others for survival and progress. This srticle explores the nature of human groups and how they have contributed to human evolution and individual freedom. The author shows how doing things together provide humans with a huge advantage over other forms of life and allowed for the development of complex, technological cultures.*

Fish gotta swim. Birds gotta fly. And people, it seems, gotta concoct a colossal array of cultural practices, group affiliations, and ethnic identities.

Over tens of thousands of years, we have acquired a special aptitude for tailoring ideas and innovations to the shifting needs of such groups, then passing the finished products onto the next generation. And in no time at all, on an evolutionary scale, urban societies and political states have become commonplace. Their astounding achievements and horrifying failures amass at an ever-quickening, often overwhelming pace.

An evolutionary process unique to our species has molded societies capable of shooting astronauts to the moon and millions of designated enemies to death, assert Peter J. Richerson of the University of California, Davis, and Robert Boyd of the University of California, Los Angeles. Cultural highs and lows alike spring from the human facility for coalescing into social units that extend far beyond family and friends, the two anthropologists argue.

In these assemblies, genetically-unrelated folks band together by adopting cultural and ethnic practices that elicit mutual good will and good samaritanism. In contrast, small groups hold together through the return of favors between individuals and threats of punishment for selfish misdeeds.

Large cultural congregations dance to a peppier evolutionary tune than the traditional Darwinian waltz, in which genetic traits useful to a species slowly move to center stage, according to Richerson and Boyd. Instead, ideas and behaviors that give some cultural groups a survival edge over rival groups jitterbug to prominence, sometimes with a push from innate human instincts and sometimes on their own.

*Excerpted from Bruce Bower, "Ultrasocial Darwinism." SCIENCE NEWS, November 25, 1995, pp. 366-367.*

Richerson and Boyd's approach builds on the proposa—first described by Richard Dawkins of Oxford University in England—that cultural evolution occurs through the widespread imitation of new ideas, fashions, and other innovations, known collectively as "memes."

"Only in the last few millennia have human societies begun to exceed, in numbers of individuals and degree of complexity, the societies of ants, termites, and corals," Richerson contends. "What's novel in the human case is our propensity for group selection driven by a cultural inheritance system that operates alongside and in interaction with genetic evolution."

In this scenario, certain cultural groups developed ideas that yielded organizational advantages over competing groups. Unprecedented levels of cooperation among hordes of genetic strangers then resulted in ultrasocial institutions and societies extending far beyond family and friends, argue Richerson and Boyd.

Cultural group selection represents an alternative to traditional notions of culture. Social scientists have long assumed that people living in different parts of the world fabricated unrelated cultural systems mainly in response to local circumstances. Most theories assume that a small number of genetically ingrained instincts, such as the hunger and sex drives, spawned a bevy of unique cultures throughout the world.

Over tens of thousands of years, cultural group selection has yielded the ultrasocial arrangements of modern life, in their view. In fact, the scientists maintain, ethnographic evidence suggests that bands of hunter-gatherers and foragers have long maintained flexible "tribal" organizations of 500 to 1,500 people, in which geographically separate groups help one another at critical junctures and share the same language and traditions. Under these circumstances, collective adaptations could have accumulated even faster than every 500 to 1,000 years, Boyd and

Richerson argue. Cultural group selection now infuses the competition between modern political parties, business firms, and other institutions within states, as well as that between states, they contend.

Members of various ultrasocial groups need some kind of signaling system through which to elicit empathy and assistance from one another, Richerson and Boyd add. Family ties and the exchange of personal favors cannot forge cooperation on so grand a scale.

Instead, cultural collectives encourage their members to acquire symbolic traits that create a sense of solidarity, the scientists assert. Group badges of this type range from body ornaments and speech dialects to detailed religious beliefs and ritual behaviors.

Symbolic markers of group membership have flourished over the past 10,000 years, Richerson and Boyd assert. In that time, the development of agriculture has drawn people into permanent settlements and permitted huge societies to flourish. Common beliefs, communication styles, and other cultural badges have underwritten the cooperative feats of modern societies, such as the construction of road networks, irrigation systems, electronic information highways, and—seemingly without famiies.

Expanding civilizations can conflict between humanity's ancient social instinct for living with relatives and friends in small groups and demands for entering into the cooperative efforts of complex cultural institutions, the researchers propose. It makes sense, they note, that ethnic identities forged over long periods still command stubborn loyalty from those living in political states of more recent origin.

Conflicts at the core of human ultrasocial groups, unlike the more smoothly run group enterprises of the honeybee hive and the termite nest, create recurring problems, Richerson contends. For instance, major political and religious institutions constantly work to suppress budding ideological heresies that vie for people's allegiances. Complex societies have often featured self-appointed godkings, brutal inquisitions, forced conversions, and other coercive methods to deal with these threats, he argues.

Utopian experiments in ultrasociality often use extreme coercion and a cult of personality surrounding leaders (for example, the former Soviet Union's Joseph Stalin) to minimize family ties, friendships and ethnic loyalties, the Davis scientist asserts. Even in democratic societies, he holds, leaders generally take some personal advantage of their power.

Richerson stands by cultural group selection as a critical, if sketchily understood, force in the rise of ultrasocial living.

"Human social instincts are certainly not adapted to live in societies numbering in the millions organized by elites that establish a great social distance between themselves and ordinary citizens," he contends. "The means by which ancient social instincts and modern cultural institutions conspire to create complex societies remains to be told."

# B. Unhappy With the Service

MIKI TANIKAWA

*Experts and politicians have waged a war against U.S. government bureaucracies for many years because of gross inefficiency and waste of money. One proposal for reform is to follow the Japanese model of organization, which we tend to assume is much more efficient. However, as this chapter in the text documents, all bureaucracies can become corrupt, wasteful, and protective of the status quo. This article analyzes problems in Japanese government bureaucracies and how citizens are protesting against them. It shows the global nature of problems inherent in large organizations.*

That which reigns from above, or okami, is how the Japanese once described their government bureaucracy. And, as befitted their elevated position, the mandarins who ran that bureaucracy were looked up to by the public. After all, these were the men who helped devise the policies and regulatory framework that carried Japan from wartime devastation to a prosperity that was the envy of the world.

But today, Japan's 500,000-strong civil service finds itself the target of growing public anger for the very reasons it was once revered: its power and authority. With Japan moving towards deregulation and economic liberalization, the bureaucracy is increasingly under pressure to release its grip on the steering-wheel of Japan Inc. Indeed, over the last two years, bureaucracy-bashing has become all the rage in an ever-widening section of Japanese society.

The change in public attitudes could have far-reaching consequences on the way Japan is governed. An opinion poll last year showed half the Japanese public doesn't trust government officials. More recently, dozens of books have flooded the bookstores, warning that government ministries pose an impediment to economic and social reforms. Private watchdogs have been exposing bureaucratic corruption, and the newspaper industry is running with the trend.

Bureaucrats, or kanryo, "are the root of many societal ills in this country," says Shunsuke Funase, a prominent consumer-rights advocate. "They are the remains of the past and no longer have any role in a society where more and more members of the public are becoming involved in issues. Yet they wield so much power."

The kanryo-bashing is developing on two .fronts: On one level, pundits are criticizing government ministries for excessive regulation and a lack of openness. Some have

*Reprinted from Miki Tanikawa, "Unhappy With the Service," FAR EASTERN ECONOMIC REVIEW, October 12, 1995, p. 32.*

targeted the Ministry of Finance in particular, criticizing it as unwieldy and resistant to change. On a more populist level, the public is challenging the perks of bureaucrats, with housewives writing letters-to-the-editor criticizing abuses of the public purse.

It's difficult to see whether any of this will translate into real change, though. Representatives from many sectors of the economy, bred on government paternalism, continue to have an interest in the bureaucratic status quo And the politicians who bridge those interests stand as an obstacle to change.

"The Ministry of Finance should be dismantled." So editorialized the September 17 edition of Japan's influential daily, *Asahi Shimbun*. The editorial criticized this most-powerful arm of the government for its long-standing ties with entrenched interests, its inability to meet new demands for infrastructure improvements, the rigid channels through which it grants subsidies and makes other expenditures. The editorial makes reference to a book by Fumihiko Igarashi of the ruling coalition's Sakigake Party. In *Dismantling of the Ministry of Finance*, Igarashi criticizes the ministry for performing too broad a range of functions, and for being unable to change its old ways.

There's been a wave of scandals involving bureaucrats. A network of civic watchdogs—private ombudsmen at the prefectural level—have revealed local governments' widespread practice of lavishly wining and dining the central-government mandarins responsible for their budgets. Taxpayers' money was used to foot lofty bills, some of which reached 120,000 yen ($1,200) per bureaucrat per evening of entertainment. Other scandals involved high-ranking officials of the Finance Ministry who wallowed in favours of various kinds, including cash, food, and overseas trips from favour-seeking businessmen.

Some observers say the kanryo-bashing has gone

too far. Many anti-bureaucracy books have "sleazy contents," says Hideyuki Tanaka, a mid-ranking bureaucrat. They're "arguing, 'you bureaucrats, get lost.' But they dodge substantive arguments including discussing alternatives to the current systems." Tanaka says that weak political leadership makes the bureaucracy stand out. "We really want politicians to exert stronger leadership on national policy. Instead, they tend to be focused on narrow interests such as building bridges and railroads in their local constituencies," he says.

"It appears that there is too much cheap criticism of the bureaucracy," says Shiro Saito, editor of the best-seller *Kanryo*, one of the more balanced books on the subject. The collection of essays—by ex-bureaucrats, among others—calls for a shift of bureaucratic responsibilities to the private sector.

Saito says politicians and industrial leaders have to take on a larger share of national leadership, initiative and responsibility. Only then can Japan depart from the perennial dominance of bureaucrats and their regulations—what Saito describes as "bureaucratic dependence."

But Saito's proposed path is blocked by the myriad business and political interests that stand closely behind the bureaucracy, protecting the rules that have favoured them. According to one survey, three out of four middle managers in leading Japanese corporations say private businesses are dependent on the bureaucracy. Indeed, Saito says the bureaucracy has been the "kind of institution that this country's industry had desired."

There's evidence of modest change in the status quo, however. Big business interests, among the prime beneficiaries of protection in the past, are now calling for deregulation. In slow economic times, the businesses see the removal of bureaucratic obstacles as a means of cost-cutting their way to economic health.

# Resource Page

## A. ULTRASOCIAL DARWINISM

### Study Questions

• Why does the author discuss cultural groups from an evolutionary perspective?
• Why do certain cultural groups develop ideas that yield organizational advantages over competing groups?
• What does the author mean by "ultrasocial groups," and how do they often participate in cultural conflict?
• If humans are predisposed to live in groups, what is the place of individuals?
• How does the author's view of groups compare to the three sociological perspectives on groups and organizations?

### Key Concepts

cultural evolution
cultural group selection
evolutionary perspective
group badges
ultrasocial groups

### Additional Resources

• Charles Horton Cooley. *Human Nature and the Social Order*. New York: Schocken Book, 1964. This sociological classic was an early attempt to show the essential role of groups in human life.
• George Homans. *The Human Group*. New York: Harcourt, Brace, Javanovich, 1950. This classic study shows the importance of group life in human affairs.
• William Kephat and William W. Zellner. *Extraordinary Groups*. 5th ed. New York: St. Martin's Press, 1994. This book provides fascinating looks at attempts to form unusual groups usually at odd with the larger society.
• Roy Payne and Cary L. Cooper. *Groups at Work*. New York: John Wiley, 1981. This book provides insight into how groups actually work.
• Cecila Ridgeway. *The Dynamics of Small Groups*. New York: St. Martin's Press, 1983. This text provides studies of interaction in small groups that can lead to competition.

## B. UNHAPPY WITH THE SERVICE

### Study Questions

• What problems do modern Japanese government bureaucracies face?
• Why do many Japanese citizens feel bureaucrats are the root of many social ills?
• What changes have critics of the bureaucracy proposed to end these abuses?
• How do problems of Japanese bureaucracy described in the reading compare to problems described in the text?
• What changes in bureaucracy might solve the problems inherent in big organizations?

### Key Concepts

bureaucracy
deregulation
kanryo
ombudsmen
status quo

### Additional Resources

• Stewart R. Clegg. *Modern Organizations*. Newbury Park, CA: Sage, 1990. A good look at organizations.
• Barbara Czarniawska-Joerges. *Exploring Complex Organizations: A Cultural Perspective*. Newbury Park, CA: Sage, 1992. A cross-cultural look at big organizations.
• Rosabeth M. Kanter. *The Change Masters: Innovations for Producivity in the American Corporation*. New York: Simon and Schuster, 1983. A classic study of how to change large organizations.
• C. Northcotte Parkinson. *Parkinson's Law*. New York: Houghton-Mifflin, 1957. This is a classic study of bureaucracy's inefficiency.
• Thomas J. Peters and Robert H. Waterman, Jr. *In Search of Excellence: Lessons from America's Best-Run Companies*. This book contains many ideas about how to solve the problems of large organizations.

# A. 'Shaming' in an Ethnic Context

SHELDON X. ZHANG

*"Shaming" is the expression of disapproval designed to evoke remorse in the wrongdoer. It has become the center of much new research and efforts to control deviance. This article reports on some of this new work by exploring ethnic differences in shaming activity. The author compares efforts to produce remorse in Asian and African-American families and discovers that they both use similar shaming tactics but for somewhat different reasons.*

John Braithwaite's book, *Crime, Shame, and Reintegration*, was called a major advance in criminology as well as in general sociological theory. The idea of using reintegrative shaming as a social control mechanism is gaining wide acceptance in Australia and New Zealand. Since 1989, New Zealand has been experimenting with "family group conferences" that replace traditional court processing of juveniles by meeting with the citizens who care most about the young offender, the victims, and their supports. In Australia, similar community accountability conferences have also been widely implemented.

The central theme of Braithwaite's book is the concept of reintegrative shaming. Historically and cross-culturally, crime is best controlled in societies where there is a strong sense of familism and communitarianism. There is a clear sense of boundary with regard to appropriate behaviors, and violations of community standards are controlled through a continued process of shaming and reintegration. Braithwaite believes that such shaming is a much more powerful weapon to control misbehavior than formal institutional sanctions. Japanese and Chinese societies, and the Australian aboriginal culture, are some of the examples he uses to make this point.

The origins of shame, according to Braithwaite, are interpersonal. It is a process of growing awareness by which children internalize their parents' standards of appropriate behavior. This concept is equivalent to the development and maintenance of conscience where feelings of shame bring into our awareness the limits of acceptable human behaviors. For a well-socialized individual, conscience delivers an anxiety response that punishes each and every involvement in deviant behavior—a more

*Excerpted from Sheldon X. Zhang, "Measuring Shaming in an Ethnic Context," BRITISH JOURNAL OF CRIMINOLOGY, Spring, 1995, pp. 248-261.*

systematic punishment than haphazard enforcement by the legal system.

For shaming to be effective, it has to be reintegrative rather than stigmatizing. These are the two ends of a continuum. Stigmatization creates outcasts. There is no acceptance or forgiveness from the community or family from which the offender was a member. Reintegrative shaming, on the other hand is "disapproval dispensed with an ongoing relationship with the offender based on respect" (Braithwaite). It is most effective in situations where there is a high level of interdependency—the family or community in which the offended is a member. Shaming focuses on the evil of the deed rather than on the offender as an evil person.

This study attempted to translate this theory into measurable variables and apply it in a quasi-experiment. As Braithwaite repeatedly points out, crimes in certain cultures (e.g. the Japanese and Chinese) are more effectively handled through informal means than formal sanctions. It would seem reasonable to examine if reintegrative shaming is used in dealing with delinquency more often within one cultural context than in others, and more importantly, how is it employed. Perhaps the differences might help explain variation in delinquency rates across ethnic-cultural lines.

The hypothesis of this study was simple: Asian-American parents would use more shaming and guilt-inducing parenting practices on their delinquent children than would African-American parents. Asian culture is heavily influenced by Confucianism, whose core is de-emphasis of the individual and maintenance of proper social order. Rules of behavior and conduct are formalized in members' roles to a greater extent than in most other cultures. Shame and loss of face are often used to reinforce adherence to these social expectations. Such a strong sense of shaming may serve as a powerful deterrent and reintegrating agency among Asian communities even within the most violent of American cities. Shaming and guilt-induction, however, are not commonly used to describe African-American culture. On the contrary, African-Americans are often portrayed as historically subject to social stigma and injustice, the type of shaming that is disintegrative in Braithwaite's terms. Because of the physical deterioration, poverty, and other urban ills in their community, African-Americans have been stigmatized and isolated more than most other ethnic minorities. How African-American parents in such an adverse social environment manage to control and supervise their delinquent children is a question worth studying. It is even more intriguing to investigate what part reintegrative shaming plays in their parenting.

Shaming in this study consists of two parts: parental shaming and communitarian shaming. Parental shaming involves practices that aim at inducing shameful or guilty feelings within the child about what he has done. Communitarian shaming is making the child's immediate social circle aware of his delinquent status. For shaming to be reintegrative, it has to take place within an ongoing interdependent relationship, in which the socially significant figures who display disapproval of the delinquent act also care about the well-being and integrity of the offender. Reintegration was thus operationalized as the extent to which the parents are involved in the child's life, are willing to forgive the incident, and believe that the child is basically good.

The hypothesized difference between the two ethnic groups was only supported by the findings on verbal shaming, which raises several issues. The first is instrument sensitivity. Asian parents were found to use significantly more verbal chastisement, which was measured by items that clearly connote shaming. The interviewers reported that most Asian parents felt ashamed of and responsible for the minor's arrest. The feeling of embarrassment and shame permeated most interviews. But to translate these observations into measurable items still remains a challenge.

Secondly, it could be that the differences between Asian-Americans and African-Americans in the ways of provoking shame and guilt to control the young are more imagined than real. We assume these two cultures share very different customs and rituals in their child-rearing practices, but few empirical efforts have been made to examine systematically how exactly they differ. In this study, it was found that being married was more responsible for the difference on verbal shaming between the two ethnic groups than any other variables, and certainly not ethnicity.

On the other hand, reports from interviewers clearly indicated that for most Asian parents being arrested was not only considered an embarrassment for the family, but also an indication of failure in parental efforts to steer the child in the right direction. Many of the Asian mothers wept as they were interviewed and expressed remorse over their son's behavior and the trouble they caused to society. Many of them viewed the fines and community service ordered by the court not only as a punishment, but as a payback to society. It was also found in this study that new immigrant Asian parents with their delinquent children born abroad were much more likely to use shaming than other parents.

Many African-American parents, however, impressed the interviewers as seeing the arrest incident as just another confrontation with the oppressive justice system. Many of them felt their sons did something wrong, but their anger and emotions were mostly aimed at external and social factors. The apparent emotional turmoil as a result of the minor's arrest was much lower than that of Asian parents, perhaps because the two ethnic groups have had very contrasting histories.

Braithwaite's theory stresses that effective crime control cannot be accomplished through de-communitized professionalization of law enforcement and a punishment-oriented justice system. Instead, public policies should try to build a cultural climate that uses reintegrative shaming to foster social obligations to comply to the law.

# B. "Just Every Mother's Angel"

### KAREN A. JOE AND MEDA CHESNEY-LIND

*The public and the media are very concerned about gangs and the widespread growth of gang violence. These groups are often portrayed as criminal and violent, and frequently in trouble with the police. However, sociologists know that gangs, like all forms of deviance, grow out of social conditions and can serve important functions. This reading reports on research done among members of gangs in Holululu, Hawaii. It notes that young men and women from diverse social situations form gangs to escape boredom and gain a sense of family.*

Official estimates of the number of youth involved in gangs have increased dramatically over the past decade. Currently, more than 90 percent of the nation's largest cities report youth gang problems, up from about half in 1983. As a result, public concern about the involvement of young men in gang activity, and the perceived violence associated with this lifestyle, has soared. The role of young men of color in these official estimates of gang activity, to say nothing of the public stereotypes of gangs, can hardly be overstated. There is a clear need, then, to balance, sharpen, and focus our analytical lenses on gender and ethnic variations in youth gang participation.

Hawaii is probably the most ethnically diverse state. The largest population groups are Japanese American (25 percent), European American (33 percent), Filipino American (13.9 percent), and Hawaiian/part-Hawaiian (17 percent). Although Hawaii is ethnically diverse, it is not without racial or ethnic tensions. Class and ethnic divisions tend to reflect the economic and political power struggles of the state's past as a plantation society as well as its current economic dependence on mainland tourism. In this mix, recent immigrants as well as the descendants of the island's original inhabitants are among the most dispossessed; consequently, youth actively involved in gangs are drawn predominantly from groups that have recently immigrated to the state (Samoans and Filipinos) or from the increasingly marginalized Native-Hawaiian population.

Like other major cities, Honolulu has witnessed a rapid growth in police estimates of gang activity and gang membership. By 1993, the number of gangs reached 171 with 1,267 members. Hawaii policy makers, concerned about the trends in gang membership, enacted legislation to develop a statewide response to youth gangs. One study of

*Excerpted from Karen A. Joe and Meda Chesney-Lind, "Just Every Mother's Angel: An Analysis of Gender and Ethnic Variations in Youth Gang Membership," GENDER AND SOCIETY, August, 1995, pp. 408-427.*

gangs, though, suggested that stereotypes regarding gang members' involvement in serious criminal behavior are just that, and underscored the need for a more qualitative understanding of gang membership among boys and girls. Toward this end, in-depth interviews with 48 self-identified gang members were conducted. Informants responded to a series of open-ended questions regarding his or her gang's history, its organization, activities, membership roles, and his or her involvement with the group, and interaction with family, the community, and the policy.

Most of the boys and all of the girls said they were attending school. The majority of the boys and girls live with both parents and are dependent on them for money—though about a third of the boys also work. About one fourth of the boys and girls reported stealing to obtain money. Their family lives are not without problems—over half of the boys are three quarters of the girls report physical abuse. In addition, 62 percent of the girls state that they have been sexually abused or sexually assaulted. Over 90 percent of the boys and three quarters of the girls were arrested, some many times. All respondents described the visible presence of gangs in their neighborhoods, and in most cases, a family member could provide them with firsthand knowledge about gangs. Virtually all of the girls and boys had a family member, usually a sibling, who belonged to a gang.

Although the interviews were done with individual gang members, it is important to know that gangs in the Islands tend to be ethnically organized and generally exclusively male or female. Filipino youth and Samoan youth tend to share the stresses of immigration; these include language difficulties, parentalization, and economic marginality. Beyond this, though, the cultures are very different. Samoan culture is heavily influenced by the Polynesian value system of collective living, communalism, and social control through family and village ties. Samoan adults drawn from this traditional, communal society experience cultural shock upon immigration when poverty forces isolation, frustration, and accommodation to a materialistic, individualistic society. As their children begin to feel caught between two very different systems of values, and as the village system of social controls weakens, the pressures and problems in Samoan families multiply.

In contrast, Filipino immigrants come from a culture that has already been affected by centuries of colonialism. As a consequence, the Philippines is a myriad of discrete ethnic cultures that have been reshaped by Spanish and U.S. conquest and occupation. One of the many costs attending colonialism, one of the most insidious is that many Filipinos feel ambivalence about the value of their own culture. Native Hawaiians have much in common with other Native-American groups as well as with African Americans. Their culture was severely challenged by the death and disease that attended contact with the West in the eighteenth century. Until very recently, Hawaiian was a dying language, and many Hawaiians were losing touch with anything that resembled Hawaiian culture.

A number of interrelated themes surfaced in the interviews with our respondents, which provide a framework for understanding youth involvement in gangs.

Generally, boys and girls have found the gang to be the most realistic solution to boredom. One respondents uniformly stated that their group provides a meaningful social outlet in an environment that has little else to offer. A sense of solidarity develops among those who face a similar plight, and as our respondents describe, their group provides a network of reliable friends who can be "counted on." Consequently, a large number of hours in school and outside of school are spent "hanging out" together and "wanting to have fun." Much of their time together is spent in social activities, particularly sports. Beyond sports, however, the social dimension of the group and the specific solutions to boredom operate differently in the lives of the girls and boys. For example, several of our female Samoan girls, indicate that they spend a great deal of their time together "harmonizing, going to dances and competitions and all that." The integration of these activities into gang life signifies an interface between traditional culture and the culture of the street. By contrast, the boys relieve the boredom and find camaraderie in the traditional sport of "cruising." Cruising in an automobile is a regular part of their life with the group, and is often accompanied by other expressions of masculinity, specifically "drinking," "fight-

ing," and "petty thieving," including "ripping off tourists."

The impact of distressed communities is felt not only by young people but by their families as well. Our respondents come from several different types of family situations. In many cases their parents are "overemployed," holding two jobs in working class occupations. Unfortunately, when both parents are struggling to stay afloat in this economy, supervision is absent in the home. A few youth indicated that they are essentially on their own. It is not surprising that these young people feel a sense of isolation and consequently find support and solace among members of their group. In sharing their problems at home with each other, the members of the group take on the role of a surrogate family. A common theme in the lives of our female and male respondents is that the gang serves as an alternative family. As Tina, a 15-year-old Samoan explains, "We all like sistas all taking care of each other." The symbolic kinship of the group is even reflected in the name of one female Samoan group called JEMA, which stands for Just Every Mother's Angel.

This article has stressed the need to explore gangs in their social context and to avoid totalizing notions of either boys' or girls' gangs. Previous research as well as our own interviews clearly suggest that such an approach is needed. One of the major conclusions one draws from listening to these young women and men is that the gang is a haven for coping with the many problems they encounter in their everyday life in marginalized communities. Paradoxically, the sense of solidarity achieved from sharing everyday life with similarly situated others has the unintended effect of drawing many gang youth into behaviors that ultimately create new problems for them.

On the broadest level, both the girls and boys are growing up in communities racked by poverty, racism, and rapid population growth. The gang is clearly a product of these factors. Shaped by the ethnicity, race, and gender of its participants, the gang takes on different shapes depending on its composition. Media constructions of gang behavior, then, which stress the violence done by gang members, need to be countered by far richer assessments of the role played by gangs in the lives of these young people. Products of distressed neighborhoods, the gangs emerge to meet many needs that established institutions do not address. Many of the impulses that propel youth into gangs are prosocial and understandable—the need for safety, security, and a sense of purpose and belonging.

# C. Social Cleansing in Colombia

PAUL JEFFERY

*Different countries define and react to deviance in many ways. In some countries, perceived deviance provokes strong reactions, leading to formal and informal ways of controlling unapproved behavior. Sometimes the efforts to control deviance becomes deviant themselves when social control agents use controversial or violent methods. This reading reports on such a case in the country of Colombia. It describes a policy of "social cleansing," where official and unofficial agents undertake inhuman policies such as gathering up prostitutes and drug users from the streets and killing them.*

Outside the morgue the pay phones weren't working, so the girl walked half a block down the street until she found one that did work. After changing a bill for some coins in a little store, she phoned her father. "They took my Jorge, they took my Jorge," she cried into the handset. As Yolanda Páez's coins were about to run out, she suggested that her parents take an offering among their neighbors to hire a marimba band for the wake. "Jorge would like that," she declared as the line went dead.

Yolanda's brother, Jorge Páez Miranda, a 19-year-old painter, met his death early on the morning of February 26 in a crime-torn section of Bogotá known as "the Bronx." Along with three other young men, Páez was shot and stabbed; the four bodies were found strewn just a few meters from Martyr's Park.

Here in this sprawling city of 7 million people, as in large cities throughout Latin America, the murder of the four young men is part of a larger plot to assassinate people that society at large has declared desechable—"disposable." Be they street children, recyclers of newspaper and glass bottles, prostitutes, petty criminals, transvestites, homosexuals, drug users or just the indigent who inhabit the region's eerie urban landscapes, they have become targets for those who seek to rid the world of the weak, the "degenerate," the surplus.

On a continent where democratically elected governments now rule from shore to shore, and neoliberal market forces are opening up the region for foreign investment, this phenomenon of "social cleansing" seems outdated, out of place, something characteristic of the Nazis or perhaps a holdover from the repressive military dictatorships that ruled in the '60s and '70s. But it exists nonetheless.

Though the details are murky, government secu-

*Excerpted from Paul Jeffrey, "Social Cleansing in Colombia," THE CHRISTIAN CENTURY, April 12, 1995, pp. 380-382*

rity forces are involved in exterminating the disposables. Twenty-four hours after the massacre in the Bronx, in the early hours of the morning, I walked through the center of Bogotá, where by day government offices bustle and by night cheap brothels and bars bustle. I strolled past people curled asleep under plastic sheeting on the sidewalk, past *cartoneros* pushing their carts full of cardboard to be sold to recyclers, past tired faces smoking cigarettes of *basuco*—cheap cocaine-in dark doorways. Every few minutes, unmarked cars-windows darkened, license plates missing—cruised along the streets. Motorcycles without plates, their riders dressed completely in black, walkie-talkies attached to their chests, roared through the urban canyons, shattering the peace of the poor, driving unchallenged past soldiers standing guard outside government buildings. The killers freely roam the streets of Bogotá with impunity.

The next day I went to El Cartucho, a desperate section of downtown Bogotá a few blocks from the Bronx. The zone is so renowned for crime and violence that no taxi driver would take me there. A man I'll call Enrique escorted me through the narrow streets. With him, I had been told, I would be relatively safe—not that the small pistol I glimpsed in his back pocket would do much good. But he was known and trusted by the street people.

As we walked by people sorting through piles of discarded shoes and collecting dirty plastic cups into gunny sacks, I asked him about the massacre of the four young men. It took a few minutes to clarify which massacre I was talking about. He told of bodies found the day before in different parts of the zone. Yet those killings hadn't made the papers; bodies were usually removed by dawn, Enrique told me, and no reporters ever asked about the dead. Yes, he had heard of the four bodies in the Bronx. When I asked him who had killed them, he looked up and down the street, then focused his weary eyes on me. "They come at night in cars or on motorcycles, all dressed in black, their faces covered," he declared. "They pull out their guns, and start shooting." He formed a machine gun with his hands and feigned a spraying of gunfire all over the street.

Walking farther, we watched a shiny four-wheel-drive Mitsubishi pull up to a nearby building. While two well-dressed men got out and went inside, two others-wearing leather jackets, carrying walkie-talkies and Uzis-remained outside, scanning the street. Enrique told me that one of the men was the head of the local police anti-drug unit, calling on a drug dealer who hadn't paid his "tax" to the police official. "They're using persuasion now," Enrique said. "But if he doesn't pay up, he and some others will be dead tomorrow morning."

The rampant corruption of Colombia's security forces combines with a general feeling of discomfort toward the poor to create a climate ripe for proponents of social cleansing. Most uncomfortable with the poor are merchants who feel harassed and threatened by the unwashed hordes of people who sometimes rob and often just scare away customers. The merchants put up the money. The soldiers and police do the killing because it earns them money and satisfies their intensified machismo.

Gómez argues that the media play a big role in fostering social cleansing, heightening the perceived threat the poor represent to the middle and upper class. "The press lies, covers up, blames the victims, helps promote the silence of the innocents," he says.

Gómez cites press coverage of the February 26 massacre in the Bronx as an example. "Within two days of the killings, the newspapers ran stories about how the four were victims of a turf war between drug gangs. I don't believe it. When did the Colombian press become such excellent investigators?"

Carlos Rojas, a researcher at Bogotá's Center for Investigation and Popular Education, a Jesuit think-tank, has studied social cleansing for several years. He says the phenomenon emerged in late 1979 with killings of prostitutes and homosexuals and has steadily grown over the years; it is carried out by a coalition of police and soldiers, paramilitary bands, merchants, politicians and civic leaders. The sponsors form death squads to do the killing, baptizing such groups with names like "Love for Medellin." According to Rojas, the killings are motivated by the groups' desire to discipline what they consider unacceptable behavior, as well as to displace or confine the popula-tion of disposable people in certain urban areas—the latter motivations clearly emerging from the interests of urban landowners and merchants. In this scenario he says, "the poor are seen by the wealthy and the government as simply superfluous, disposable."

In the past seven years, using official police reports and press clippings, Rojas has documented some 2,000 cases of social cleansing nationwide; even so, he and Gómez contend, many cases go unreported. "Many of the dead don't pass through the morgue," says Gómez. "I've seen garbage trucks leave the center of the city early in the morning with body parts sticking out from the trash. And some funeral parlors make money on the side by taking cadavers from social-cleansing operations and making them disappear. Some use tanks of acid. A whole industry of social cleansing has developed here, much like what happened with the Nazis."

During the week the family of Jorge Páez morned his death with marimba music, Colombia was a frequent topic of discussion in Washington—but not for the right reasons. Capitol Hill was beginning another war of words about whether certain countries should be "certified" as allies in the war on drugs, and Colombia was frequently chastised for not cooperating fully in the fight against narcotrafficking. The emotional rhetoric about narcotrafficking is, according to Ricardo Esquivia, a "smokescreen to divert attention from the real issues that affect Colombia." The problem here is less the war on drugs than the war against the poor. Whatever threatens the armed capitalism of the Colombian elite is dealt with harshly. And given the 97 percent rate of impunity for crimes committed in Colombia, no one will be punished. Unless the U.S., Columbia's strongest ally and largest trading partner, modifies its relationship with this country, in places like the Bronx and El Cartucho, as well as in isolated rural communities where poor peasants struggle for recognition of their basic rights, the body count will continue to grow.

# Resource Page

## A. SHAMING IN AN ETHNIC CONTEXT

### Study Questions

• What is reintegrative shaming and why is it important?
• How did the author untertake research to measure shaming in an ethnic context?
• What were some of the different ways Asian and African-American families undertake the practice of shaming?
• How did all of the families the author studies perform reintegrative shaming in similar ways?

### Key Concepts

Confucianism
reintegrative shaming
social stigmatization

### Additional Resources

• Howard Becker. *Outsiders*. New York: Free Press, 1963. A set of studies on persons labeled deviant.
• John Braithwaite. *Crime, Shame, and Reintegration*. New York: Cambridge University Press, 1989. The basic text.
• W. Gove. *The Labeling of Deviance: Evaluating a Perspective*. Newbury Park, CA: Sage, 1980. A text that shows problems in the labeling perspective.

## B. EVERY MOTHER'S ANGEL

### Study Questions

• Why does the reading's authors feel that much research on gangs reflects stereotypes?
• Who did the authors interview, and what did they discover?
• What specific social situations seem to give rise to participation in gangs?
• Based on the reading, how might the U.S. develop a more comprehensive response to the gang problem?

### Key Concepts

• camarderie
• marginalization
• Pacifric Island culture
• social outlet

### Additional Resources

• Richard Cloward and Lloyd Ohlin. *Delinquency and Opportunity*. New York: Free Press, 1960. A classic.
• Luis Rodriquez. *Always Running: Gang Days in L.A.* New York: Simon & Schuster, 1993. A personal account of life in a gang.
• Terry Williams. *The Cocaine Kids*. Reading, MA: Addison Wesley, 1989. A great study of a drug gang.

## C. SOCIAL CLEANSING IN COLOMBIA

### Study Questions

• What is social cleansing, and what is its purpose?
• Who are the persons selected for removal from the streets?
• Why is the "social cleansing" policy a form of deviant behavior?
• What efforts are underway to curb social cleansing in Colombia?

### Key Concepts

the *desechable*
narcotrafficking
social cleansing
social control

### Additional Resources

• Nanette J. Davis and Clarice Stasz. *Social Control of Deviance*. New York: McGraw-Hill, 1990. A good treatment of social control.
• Scott B. MacDonald. *Dancing on a Volcano: The Latin American Drug Trade*. New York: Praeger, 1988. Good background on drugs.
• Lucien Bodard. *Green Hell*. New York: Dutton, 1972. A account of a serious case of social cleansing, and some reasons why it occurs.

# A. To Have and Have Not

MICHAEL LIND

*Social class is a dimension of society that cuts across ethnic and racial lines. Class refers to the distribution of rewards in society, or "the haves and the have nots," and reflects the economic structure of a society. This reading examines the ongoing conflict between the rich and poor in the U.S. and shows how political parties and race cloud the basic and growing class divisions in U.S. society.*

Judging by the headlines that have been leading the news for the last several years, public debate in the United States at the end of the twentieth century has become a war of words among the disaffected minorities that so often appear on the neverending talk show jointly hosted by Oprah, Larry King, Jenny Jones, and the McLaughlin Group. Conservatives at war with liberals; Christian fundamentalists at odds with liberal Jews; blacks at war with whites; whites at war with Hispanic immigrants; men at war with women; heterosexuals at war with homosexuals; and the young at war with the old. A guide to the multiple conflicts in progress would resemble the personals pages in the Village Voice, with "versus" or "contra" substituted for "seeking" (Pro-Sex Classicists versus Anti-Sex Modernists).

The noise is deceptive. Off-camera, beyond the blazing lights, past the ropy tangle of black cords and down the hall, in the corner offices (on Capitol Hill as well as at General Electric, The Walt Disney Company, and CBS News), people in expensive suits quietly continue to go about the work of shifting the center of gravity of wealth and power in the United States from the discounted many to the privileged few. While public attention has been diverted to controversies as inflammatory as they are trivial—Should the Constitution be amended to ban flag-burning? Should dirty pictures be allowed on the Internet?—the American elites that subsidize and staff both the Republican and Democratic parties have steadfastly waged a generation-long class war against the middle and working classes. Now and then the television cameras catch a glimpse of what is going on, as they did last year during the NAFTA and GATT debates, when a Democratic President and a bipartisan majority in Congress collaborated in the sacrifice of American labor to the interests of American corporations and foreign capital. More recently, with a candor rare among politicians, House Speaker Newt Gingrich argued against raising the minimum wage in the United States on

*Excerpted from Michael Lind, "To Have and Have Not," HARPER'S MAGAZINE, June, 1995, pp. 35-39.*

the grounds that a higher minimum wage would handicap American workers in their competition with workers in Mexico.

The camera, however, quickly returns to the set and the shouting audience, while assistant producers hold up placards with the theme for the day: the Contract with America, the New Covenant, Affirmative Action, Moral Renewal. It's against the rules to talk about a rapacious American oligarchy, and the suggestion that the small group of people with most of the money and power in the United States just might be responsible to some degree for what has been happening to the country over the last twenty years invariably invites the news media to expressions of wrath and denial. Yes, the pundits admit, economic and social inequality have been growing in the United States, with alarming results, but the ruling and possessing class cannot be blamed, because, well, there is no ruling and possessing class.

The American oligarchy spares no pains in promoting the belief that it does not exist, but the success of its disappearing act depends on equally strenuous efforts on the part of an American public anxious to believe in egalitarian fictions and unwilling to see what is hidden in plain sight. Anybody choosing to see the oligarchy in its native habitat need do nothing else but walk down the street to an office tower housing a major bank, a corporate headquarters or law firm, or a national television station. Enter the building and the multiracial diversity of the street vanishes as abruptly as the sound of the traffic. Step off the elevator at the top of the tower and apart from the clerical and maintenance staff hardly anybody is non-white. The contrast between the street and the tower is the contrast between the grass roots and the national headquarters, the field office and the home office. No matter what your starting point, the closer you come to the centers of American politics and society, the more everyone begins to look the same. Though corporate executives, shop stewards, and graduate-student lecturers could not be more different, the people who run big business bear a remarkable resemblance to the people who run big labor, who in turn might be mistaken for the people in charge of the media and the universities. They are the same people. They differ in their opinions—and in almost no other way. Almost exclusively white, disproportionately mainline Protestant or Jewish, most of the members of the American elites went to one of a dozen Ivy League colleges or top state universities. Not only do they have advanced professional or graduate degrees—J.D.'s, M.B.A.'s, Ph.D.s, M.D.'s—but usually at least one of their parents (and sometimes both) has advanced professional or graduate degrees. They dress the same. They talk the same. They walk the same. They have the same body language, the Same gestures. They eat the same food, drink the same drinks, and play the same sports. They read the same publications.

Along with their dependents, to about 20 percent of the population, this relatively new and still evolving political and social oligarchy is not identified with any particular region of the country. Homogeneous and no-madic, the overclass is the first truly national upper class in American history. In a managerial capitalist society like our own, the essential distinction is not between the "bourgeoisie" (the factory owners) and the "proletariat" (the factory workers) but between the credentialed minority (making a living from fees or wages supplemented by stock options) and the salaried majority. The salaried class-at-will employees, lacking a four-year college education, paid by the hour, who can be fired at any time, constitutes the real middle class, accounting, as it does, for three-quarters of the population.

The most remarkable thing about our own American oligarchy is the pretense that it doesn't constitute anything as definite as a social class. We prefer to assign good fortune to our individual merit, saying that we owe our perches in the upper percentiles of income and education not to our connections but solely to our own I.Q., virtue, or genius. Had we been switched at birth by accident, had we grown up in a ghetto or barrio or trailer park, we would have arrived at our offices at ABC News or the Republican National Committee or the ACLU in more or less the same amount of time. The absence of black and Hispanic Americans in our schools and our offices and our clubs can only be explained, we tell ourselves, not by our extrinsic advantages but by their intrinsic defects. What other explanation for their failure to rise can there be? America, after all, is a classless society.

Or rather a two-class society. The belated acknowledgment of an "underclass" as a distinct group represents the only exception to the polite fiction that everyone in the United States, from a garage mechanic to a rich attorney (particularly the rich attorney), belongs to the "middle class." Over the past decade the ghetto poor have been the topic of conversation at more candlelight-and-wine dinner parties than I can recall, but without looking at the program or the wine list it is impossible to tell whether one is among nominal liberals or nominal conservatives. The same kind of people in the same kind of suits go on about "the blacks" as though a minority within a 12 percent minority were taking over the country, as if Washington were Pretoria and New York a suburb of Johannesburg. Not only do the comfortable members of the overclass single out the weakest and least influential of their fellow citizens as the cause of all their sorrows but they routinely, and preposterously, treat the genuine pathologies of the ghetto-high levels of violence and illegitimacy as the major problems facing a country.

During the past generation, the prerogatives of our new oligarchy have been magnified by a political system in which the power of money to buy TV time has become a good deal more important than the power of labor unions or party bosses to mobilize voters. Supported by the news media, which it largely owns, the oligarchy has waged its war of attrition against the wage-earning majority on several fronts: regressive taxation, the expatriation of industry, and mass immigration.

Although the inequalities of income in the United States are now greater than at any time since the 1930s, and although numerous observers have remarked on the fact and cited abundant statistics in support of their observations, the response of the American overclass has been to blame everybody but its nonexistent self—to blame the ghetto, or the schools, or the liberal media, or the loss of family values.

In any other democracy, an enraged citizenry probably would have rebelled by now against a national elite that weakens unions, slashes wages and benefits, pits workers against low-wage foreign and immigrant competition—and then informs its victims that the chief source of their economic problems is a lack of "high personal diligence." But for whom could an enraged citizen vote? The American overclass manages to protect itself from popular insurgencies, not only through its ownership of the news media but also by its financial control of elections and its use of affirmative-action patronage.

# B. Hong Kong's Underclass Struggles to be Heard

SHELLA TEFFT

*Asian economies are among the fastest growing in the world, and we think of Japan, Korea and Hong Kong as countries with little poverty and growing wealth. But sometimes the changes created by economic progress dislocates farmers and workers and can lead to poverty. This reading examines how an underclass has emerged in Hong Kong, which is one of the richest areas of the world. Like the U.S., this underclass is made up of the elderly, dislocated workers and recent immigrants. The reading also documents the insensitivity of the wealthy and government to the plight of the poor.*

> *There are 800,000 of us in Hong Kong.*
> *We are not lazy,*
> *Retired life is very hard.*
> *Many of us are sick and hungry.*
> *The government does not care.*
> *But we solve these problems by joining to fight,*
> *Heart-to-Heart, for elderly rights.*
> **Elderly Rights Rap**

Leading dozens of elderly in a self-penned rap song for decent housing and care, Ho Hei-wah was staging one of his many rallies for Hong Kong poor.

In this affluent British colony, Mr. Ho's appeals to help thousands of unemployed, aged, and immigrants living at the margin of Hong Kong's prosperity stir little sympathy and even provoke irritation.

"Among a populace of free wheeling entrepeneurs and capitalists, increasing numbers are being left behind in the chase to make money," says the social woker. " For many of those who emigrated from China, helped build the colony with their labor, and still struggle for better lives, this is unfair," he says.

"Many of these people came alone to Hong Kong in the 1950s and '60s, worked hard, and provided a cheap labor force for industry," says Ho, director of the grass-roots Society for Community Organization. "For 30 years, there was no labor laws and the government rejected them for pension schemes. Finally, when they are old and can no longer work, they end up living in poverty in [slums]."

Amid the glittlre and bustle of one of the world's wealthiest enclaves, a poverty-striken underclass struggles

*Reprinted from Shella Tefft, "Hong Kong's Underclass Struggles to Be Heard," THE CHRISTIAN SCIENCE MONITOR, November 29, 1995, pp. 12, ff.*

to be heard in Hong Kong. With an unparalleled number of millionaires, the British colony boasted a per capita gross domestic product of $21,700 in 1994, the 13th highest in the world—exceeding those of Japan, Singapore, or Great Britain. But Hong Kong, which reverts to Chinese rule in 1997, has one of the widest gaps between rich and poor. According to a government survey the poorest 20 percent of Hong Kong's households earn less than 5 percent of the colony's income; the top 20 percent account for more than half of all income.

Although poverty in Hong Kong doesn't begin to match that of China, India, and other Asian countries, official figures from 1991 show a median monthly income of $3,460 for the bottom 20 percent of Hong Kong households compared to $27,965 for the richest 20 percent.

Economists say the gap is widening as Hong Kong's economy shifts from manufacturing to service, factory jobs are lost to lower-cost China, and inflation runs at more than 9 percent. Almost three-quarters of the economy is now in the service sector.

"Income inequality is worsening," says Tsang Shu-ki, an economist at Hong Kong Baptist University. "A major factor is that remuneration in the service sectors is more unequal than in the manufacturing industries."

Hong Kong's budding democracy, spurred by controversial political reforms pushed through by British Governor Chris Patten, has given a voice to financially-strapped respondents worried about unemployment, run-down public housing, and inadequate welfare assistance.

During the last two years, Hong Kong's welfare rolls have jumped by one-third, to more than 110,000. The government's scramble to build new public housing is failing to keep pace with demand. And authorities are pledging to overhaul the welfare system under which an elderly resident only gets $240 per month to live on, more than half of which must go to pay public housing costs.

In the last two decades, dozens of new grass-roots organizations have emerged to amplify the concerns of the poor. Ho, the social worker, is among the most vocal in demanding the government do more for the downtrodden. His crusades have earned him a prominent public profile as well as the distrust of many in Hong Kong, including government leaders, businessmen, and even fellow democracy activists with whom he has disagreed over style and political issues. Enjoying the colony's laissez-faire climate, many residents resent contributing to an old-age pension scheme for Hong Kong's elderly.

"To stand up for the underdog here takes real guts," says a Hong Kong business leader who asked not to be identified. "In a capitalist community like Hong Kong, people are successful because of their own abilities. If you are a loser in the game, it's your fault." Ho's advocacy of illegal immigrants from China has set him at odds with the authorities and labor unions worried about unemployment. Ten years ago, he helped the wives of immigrant fishermen whose boats were being blocked by police as they tried to enter Hong Kong. Of late, he assisted a six-year-old boy expelled from Hong Kong when his parents couldn't prove he was born in the territory.

"In recent years, I have started working with illegal immigrants because they suffer from low [immigration] quotas and corruption," says the affable social worker who has an easy laugh and a passion for powerful motorcycles. "The Hong Kong people support most of my work except that for the illegal immigrants. Sometimes, on the street, people stop me and say they support me. But they say I should stop helping the immigrants."

Regularly, he embarrasses the government by leading marches of elderly people forced to live in what are known as "cages"—dormitories with six-foot-tall metal cages stacked in rows. He helped persuade United Nations human rights officials to visit Hong Kong to investigate the plight of the 4,000 people estimated to live in such conditions.

Indeed, housing is an increasingly explosive issue among the colony's underclass. About 159,000 families live in makeshift huts or squalid tenements as they endure up to a seven-year wait for public housing. The authorities are trying to force out legions of residents who stay in highly subsidized public apartments but own property elsewhere.

In September, Mr. Patten, the British governor, was shoved by an angry mob of 1,000 residents during a tour of a flooded temporary slum.

Ho maintains there are thousands of poor struggling to make ends meet among the 1.4 million Hong Kong residents living in substandard housing.

"I organized these people and bring their problems to the desk of the government. Otherwise, the officials don't want to see the problem," says Ho, who is unmarried and lives in public housing himself with his grandmother.

Ho says his family worries that his advocacy for the destitute and jobless and activism in human rights puts him on a collision course with China, which will take over Hong Kong in two years. As chairman of the Hong Kong Human Rights Commisison, he traveled to the United States last summer as a guest of the government to meet American activists and leaders.

"When you talk to poor people about 1997, the feeling is very mixed. They don't like the British government because they have suffered under this system. They know the British government is making a profit but doesn't want to share," he says. "But they also know the Chinese government won't help them either. So they never think about next week."

# C. African Welfare Systems in Perspective

*JAYIWOLA ERINOSHO*

*This chapter in the text analyzes the U.S.' beliefs about welfare and the ongoing effort to reform the welfare system. However, confusion and strong feelings about the poor have led to an inconclusive debate about how to change welfare. This reading might help clarify aspects of the debate by looking at welfare systems in another culture. It traces the evolution of welfare in Africa, where traditional and modern social welfare philosophies exist side by side.*

The type of welfare system which a society has for its sick and needy members depends on its stage of development. Because various strands of help are regarded as social welfare or social security, they usually follow trends of economic development. When a society was at a rudimentary stage of development such as in classical and medical times in Europe, or in pre-colonial and colonial Africa, the welfare of those who were poor and incapable of sustenance was taken up by the extended network and the community at large through the instrumentalities of norms of kinship. Traditional societies have there always found ways of caring for their less fortunate and less endowed members through redistribution and reciprocal forms of exchange.

The scope and coverage of social welfare generally follow the pattern of socio-economic development in the countries concerned. Just as they are related to the pattern of economic change, so also are they to socio-demographic changes such as alteration in the occupational and age structure of the population.

The scope of a typical highly developed social welfare system covers physical risks and macro as well as microeconomic risks. Under the physical risks are old-age, invalidity, illness, accidents and death. Unemployment comes under macroeconomic risk while family burdens make up the microeconomic risk. These risks serve as the basis for the design of different social welfare programs. To cater for physical risks, such programs as old-age, invalidity and survivor schemes, work-injury compensation, as well as medical and sickness programs, exist in varying degrees in the majority of the countries of the world. There are also, in the case of economic risks, family allowance and public assistance programs.

The evolution of social welfare systems in Africa is, to some extent, analogous to what happened in Europe

*Excerpted from Jayiwola Erinosho, "African Welfare Systems in Perspective," UNESCO COURIOR, 1994, pp. 247-254*

several centuries ago. Following changes in the means and forms of production, social welfare, which was traditionally provided by the family network, was either taken over or complemented by other agents, such as ecclesiastical agencies or guilds responsible for the weak and needy. Urban-based ethnic and voluntary associations began to play such a focal role along with extended family networks in the wake of colonial rule in Africa.

However, the colonial powers began to expand social welfare programs to their overseas territories during the colonial era. The programs were initially designed to cater for European workers in the colonies. The restriction of welfare programs to these workers and state officials was largely because they were expatriates without the benefits of the indigenous cultural support system which was then available to the local population.

Social welfare programs were later extended to cover the indigenous population, most especially urban-based African workers who were uprooted from their normal surroundings by industrialization, and who were totally unprotected against the risks of life. The initiative to extend those measures to the African population was motivated by the need to stabilize the indigenous manpower available to the colonial authorities, and was also partly due to the struggle of trade unions, which in colonial times, "sought equality of rights with workers in the colonizing country, who were then the only ones covered by social security."

The extent and coverage of social welfare broadened with the attainment of nationhood in a majority of African countries in the 1960s. This was not only because the promise of widespread social welfare formed a principle means of mobilization for decolonization and thus underpinned the very legitimacy of the post-colonial state, but also because the bureaucracies of the new states ballooned, multiplying the number of wage earners directly in need of one or another form of social welfare. However, what achievements are visible for social welfare programs in Africa still fall far short of demand. For social welfare programs for the weak and needy in Africa remain an inadequate complement to the traditional modes of support which, in spite of industrialization and urbanization remain the more dominant.

The scope and coverage of social welfare programs can readily be appraised in the context of African social structure. In nearly all independent Africa, the social structure is characterized on the one hand by an amorphous and hardly regulated informal sector, and on the other by a strong, highly-regulated, organized and burgeoning public sector.

Zimbabwe typifies the case of developing African countries with a social security system which is limited in scope. Before 1976, the only form of old-age pension payable in the country was the non-contributory pension to non-Africans above the age of 60 by the then colonial government of Rhodesia. Rather than the scheme being extended to the indigenous population when the country gained independence in 1980, it was stopped in April of that year. The other form of old-age pensions is the Occupation Pension Scheme which began in 1976. Funds for this are contributed equally by employees and employers.

What goes by the way of invalidity and survivor scheme in Zimbabwe can be found under the workmen and compensation. This covers workers (excluding casual and domestic workers) who are injured or permanently disabled as a result of occupational accidents and diseases. In the case of death arising therefrom, the dependents of such victims are given some compensation. Apart from Zimbabwe, 41 other African countries had, by 1977, adopted legislation on old-age pension. The scheme is confined to wage earner but still leaves the vast majority of the population without protection of any kind. Invalidity and survivor schemes are found in 36 to 40 countries in Africa. The majority of such schemes are linked to an old-age pension scheme with roughly the same pattern.

In conclusion, these observations underscore the fact that a comprehensive social security system which covers all citizens within the formal and informal sectors/sub-sectors of the economy is yet to be articulated in several African countries. One major reason for this is the stage of development of these countries. While individuals in permanent employment are provided for, those within the informal sector are usually not covered. For the latter, the extended family networks and ethnic associations provide succor.

There is no doubt that African countries have achieved a great deal since the social welfare systems were first introduced by the colonial authorities. The rapid modernization success in Africa is bringing about a dramatic shift from a social security system which was basically anchored on the extended family network to one that is organized and sponsored by the state. One of the major achievements of social security systems in post-colonial Africa is the consolidation and expansion of schemes which were not in place by the erstwhile colonial authorities. Today, African countries have sought to modernize and implement various novel schemes within the limits of their capacity and resources.

However, this achievement is overshadowed by a number of shortcomings. Existing social welfare systems in Africa are biased in favor of the elites and the urban-based, with the rural dwellers as well as the non-literate who constitute the majority in the population in these countries uncatered for. Underdeveloped societies in transition such as those found in Africa are characterized by unequal development among social and ethnolinguistic sub-groups, and between one region of the country and the other. This situation is reflected in the landscape of social welfare. Medicare which is regarded as the pillar of the social security system in any society can be cited as an example. Nearly all major sophisticated or even well-equipped health care facilities, and highly skilled health manpower, are located in the urban centers where the elite reside. Because of this, urban centers are more endowed and their dwellers, most especially the elite among them, are better catered for than the vast majority of the non-literate in the rural and urban areas.

This trend is having serious consequences, as Africa is beginning to witness mass urban and rural poverty, including destitution among the old and the young. The growing band of destitutes which is the result of the gradual breakdown of the extended family networks in the context of a modernizing economy, and the failure of national authorities to organize a comprehensive social security system is a serious problem facing the continent today. Therefore, the failure to address redistribution of income and to relieve mass poverty through a suitable and comprehensive social security system can be viewed as a serious shortcoming.

# Resource Page

## A. TO HAVE AND HAVE NOT

### Study Questions

• What basic change in the "center of gravity of wealth and power" does this article discuss?
• How is the growth of the elite's wealth and power hidden by current debates over race and gender?
• How do both major political parties cater to the same elite social class?
• What social tensions and problems have and will arrive from these new class divisions?

### Key Concepts

egalitarian
oligarchy
overclass

### Additional Resources

• James Curtis and Lorne Tepperman. *Haves and Have-Nots*. Englewood Cliffs, NJ: Prentice-Hall, 1994. An excellent reader on current patterns of stratification.
• Mickey Kaus. *The End of Equality*. New York: Basic Books, 1992. This book more completely analyzes the changes discussed in this reading.
• Katherine S. Newman. *Falling From Grace*. New York: Vintage Books, 1988. An account of the decline of social mobility among the middle class.

## B. HONG KONG'S UNDERCLASS STRUGGLES TO BE HEARD

### Study Questions

• How has Hong Kong become one of the world's wealthiest cities?
• Who make up Hong Kong's proverty-striken underclass, and how poor are its members?
• What are some events and causes that led to the creationof this underclass?

### Key Concepts

entrepeneurs
laissez-faire
Society for Community Organization
underclass

### Additional Resources

• Ken Aulette. *The Underclass*. New York: Random House, 1982. This book invented the concept of underlass.
• James Fallows. *Looking At the Sun: The Rise of the New East Asian Economic and Political System*. New York: Pantheon Books, 1994. A good treatment of the forces giving rise to poverty and wealth in the Far East.
• C. P. Lo. *Hong Kong*. New York: Halsted Press, 1992. An analysis of the city of Hong Kong.

## C. AFRICAN WELFARE SYSTEMS IN PERSPECTIVE

### Study Questions

• What is a "welfare scheme," and what kinds of needs does it cover?
• Generally, how have welfare programs evolved in Africa?
• How do persons in the informal economy not provided with pensions and medicare take care of their needs?
• What is the major problems faced by welfare programs in most African countries?

### Key Concepts

African social structure
social welfare schemes
income redistribution

### Additional Resources

• Clin Trumbell. *The Lonly African*. Garden City, NY: Doubleday, 1963. A treatment of Africa's problems.
• William Trattner. *From Poor Law to Welfare State*, 4th ed. New York: Free Press, 1990. An excellent history of social welfare in the U.S.
• Francis Fox Piven and Richard Cloward. *Regulating the Poor*, 2nd ed. New York: Vintage Book, 1994. An excellent analysis of the functions of social welfare.

# A. Indian-Asian Americans

MARCIA MOGELONSKY

*Beginning in the 1980s, the U.S. experienced an unusually large migration of people from all over the world with as many as 20 million new persons arriving in this country. One of the most interesting groups comes from Pakistan and Bangladesh, which are parts of India geographically and ethnically close to Asia. This reading describes some features and contributions of this largely affluent group.*

Imagine a rapidly growing ethnic group of almost 1 million people who are generally well-educated and wealthy. Best of all, they speak English. Some may call this a marketer's dream. It also happens to be the general profile of Asian-Indian Americans, a segment of the population worth a closer look.

The number of Asian Indians immigrating to the United States increased rapidly after 1965, when amendments to the Immigration and Nationality Act made it possible for them to enter the country in greater numbers than ever before. Although the first sizable group of Asian Indians arrived in this country between 1907 and 1914, the population today is still primarily first-generation immigrants.

Although immigration data have been available for decades, the U.S. decennial census did not enumerate the Asian-Indian population separately from a miscellaneous category of "other Asians" until 1980. Furthermore, the population fluctuates as temporary residents arrive and leave as students, management trainees, and visiting technology specialists. As of 1990, however, the Asian-Indian population in the United States numbered 815,000, up 111 percent from 387,000 in 1980.

Asian Indians traditionally have flocked to the Northeast, and primarily the urban portions of New York and New Jersey. But California led the states in 1990, with almost 159,000 Asian-Indian residents, up from 60,000 in 1980. Wyoming boasts the smallest population of Asian Indians-240-but it is also the first state in the nation to elect an Asian Indian to its legislature, Republican Nimi McConigley. Throughout the U.S., well-educated Asian Indians are assuming positions of power.

In many cases, the first wave of an immigrant group consists of affluent people. Asian Indians are a classic example of this rule. Among Asian Indians in

*Excerpted from Marica Mogelonsky, "Asian-Indian Americans," AMERICAN DEMOGRAPHICS, August, 1995, pp. 33-37.*

the work force in 1990, 30 percent were employed in professional specialty occupations, compared with 13 percent of all U.S. employees. Twenty percent of foreign-born Indian professionals are physicians, 26 percent are engineers, and 12 percent are post-secondary teachers, according to the Washington, D.C.-based Center for Immigration Studies. Asian Indians are slightly over-represented among managerial and sales/technical/clerical workers, and under-represented among service and blue-collar workers, according to the 1990 census.

"The earlier immigrants came because of their qualifications. They had no trouble getting green cards or professional posts," says Dr. Madhulika Khandelwal of the Asian/American Center at Queens College in Flushing, New York. Indeed, foreign-born Indian professionals are highly qualified: more than 67 percent hold advanced degrees. And 21 percent of the 14,000 American-born Asian Indians aged 25 and older hold post-bachelor's degree accreditation.

"The more recent immigrants differ in two ways," says Khandelwal. "The professionals among them, those with master's degrees or even medical degrees or doctorates, are not always able to find jobs in their chosen professions in this country. They are faced with a choice-staying in India and working as professionals, or emigrating to America and working in trade or service jobs that may not suit their qualifications." "This second wave also includes lower-middle-class Indians who tend to work in service industries, usually with members of their extended families," says Khandelwal.

United States immigration policy is based on family reunification, so it is not surprising that the qualifications of immigrants have changed over the past decade, according to the Center for Immigration Studies. Many find positions in family-run businesses or work in service industries such as taxi driving until they make enough money to pursue more lucrative ventures. More than 40 percent of New York City's 40,000 licensed Yellow Cab drivers are South Asian Indians, Pakistanis, and Bangladeshis. But most see their taxi-driving phase as a transitional period to acclimatize them to the U.S. and to give them the money they need to get started.

Many Asian Indians are self-employed. The number of Asian-Indian-owned businesses increased 120 percent between 1982 and 1987, according to the latest available Survey of Minority-Owned Business Enterprises released by the Census Bureau. Dollar receipts for these businesses increased 304 percent in the same five-year period.

"Asian Indians dominate in some trades, such as convenience and stationery stores," says Eliot Kang of the New York City based Kang and Lee Advertising, which specializes in marketing to Asian minorities. Kang points out that Asian-Indian retailers get an edge on competitors by pooling their resources and forming associations, which enables them to buy in bulk and sell at lower prices. "Large family networks and family financing give these businesses a chance to grow and expand. And because so many family members are involved, Asian-Indian businesses can flourish in labor-intensive service industries."

The Census Bureau tallied close to 30,000 Asian-Indian-owned service businesses in 1987. Retail establishments ran a distant second, at slightly more than 9,000. Asian-Indian ownership of hotels and motels is the standout example of Indian penetration into the service segment. In 1994, 7,200 Asian-Indian owners operated 12,500 of the nation's 28,000 budget hotels and motels, according to the Atlanta-based Asian American Hotel Owners Association.

The median income for Asian-Indian households is $44,700, versus $31,200 for all U.S. households, according to the 1990 census. Not all Asian Indians are affluent, however. Dr. Arun Jain, professor of marketing at the State University of New York in Buffalo, divides the market into three distinct segments. The first, the majority of whom immigrated in the 1960s, is led by a cohort of highly educated men who came to this country because of professional opportunities. Most are doctors, scientists, academics, and other professionals who are now in their 50s and at the peak of their earning potential. Jain estimates that their average annual income may top $100,000. The wives of these high-powered professionals usually do not work outside of the home and are not highly educated. These women may have no more than a high school education, and a good portion do not speak English fluently, says Jain. Among

this group, the majority of children are in college or about to marry and start families of their own.

The second segment includes immigrants who came to the U.S. in the 1970s. Like the first segment, the men are highly educated professionals. Yet unlike the first wave, many are married to highly educated women who work outside of the home. Their children are college-bound teenagers.

The third segment is made up of relatives of earlier immigrants who have been sponsored by established family members in this country. They are often less well educated than members of the first two segments. This is the group most likely to be running motels, small grocery stores, gas stations, or other ventures. In this group, Jain also includes the majority of Asian-Indian Ugandans who fled that regime in the 1980s and have established themselves in this country.

Lifestyle and generational differences set the three groups apart, at least to some extent. People in the first segment are thinking about their children's marriages, while those in the second are about to put their children through college. Men in the first segment may be looking toward retirement, while the men and women in the third group are trying to establish themselves in successful businesses.

Generational distinctions are only part of the story, however. India has nearly 1 billion residents separated into 25 states and 7 union territories, speaking 15 official languages. "We are like Europe," says Pradip Kothal, president of the Iselin, New Jersey-based Indian Business Association, a not-for-profit organization linking the more than 60 small businesses that flourish in this heavily Indian enclave of Middlesex County.

Linguistic, nationalistic, and generational differences may divide the Indian population, but they share a number of underlying principles and goals. Jain points out that all Asian Indians place great value in education. "Indians will do anything to further their children's education," he says.

Financial security is also important. Saving money is a major part of Indian culture, and targeted saving-for education or retirement-is especially emphasized. Jain estimates that the savings rate among Asian Indians in the U.S. is higher than the national average of 5 percent; he places it as high as 15 to 20 percent, similar to the rate in India. Asian-Indian Americans also place a high value on inheritance and prize investments that guarantee a secure future for children and grandchildren.

# B. What Should We Call People?

HAROLD L. HODGKINSON

*The text's Chapter 8 on "Race and Ethnicity" emphasizes the social nature of race, where people are assigned to a racial category not because of actual difference but by public opinion. The definition of race therefore varies from one society to another. This reading discusses this idea by examing the different definitions of race proposed for the census in the year 2000. The author describes the unscientific mature of these definitions and proposes t the census focus on poverty, not race.*

The impending debate over the definition of race to be used in the U.S. Census for the year 2000 could be the most divisive debate over racial issues since the 1960s. In this article I will attempt to explain the problem, review its history, and examine the options for the future.

In the U.S. the answer to this question of what we should call people is not as crystal clear to the Office of Management and Budget (OMB), reporting to the House Committee on Post Office and Civil Service, Subcommittee on Census, Statistics, and Postal Personnel. While this subcommittee does not represent the most desirable political plum in the Congress, it has been at the center of a swirling debate on the nature of racial designations, as seen in hearings that began in 1993 and continued into 1994, though they were virtually ignored by the news media. Since 1977, the racial/ethnic categories that can be used on all federal forms have come from OMB Statistical Directive 15, which allows only four racial groups, designated by the following headings: American Indian/Alaskan Native; Asian/Pacific Islander; Black; and White. Ethnicity is broken down into Hispanic and non-Hispanic. These are the categories that are used on application forms for jobs, on school enrollment forms, on mortage applications, and on college scholarship and loan applications.

When we read that 18% of a state's population is black, Hispanic, Asian, or Native American, we have to assume that everyone in the category belongs completely in that box. The fact is that, on direct measurement, the darkest quarter of the white population is darker than the lightest quarter of the black population. Although racial data sound very scientific the reality is that the categories are entirely subjective. Even some trained anthropologists have argued that there are three "races," while others have argued for 37 races. Stephen Thernstrom calls this "the figment of the pigment.""

*Excerpted from Harold L. Hodgkinson, "What Should We Call People?" PHI DELTA KAPPAN, October, 1995, pp. 173-`78.*

Even if we grant that the intention of the OMB was simply to offer neutral, nonscientific statistical descriptions for use in the Census, not to create or define "race": that is precisely what Directive 15 has done for most Americans. The fact that "Hispanic" has become widely used only in the last 20 years is due in large part to the fact that the term entered the Census lexicon in 1970. (When the Census form mentioned "South Americans" as a category, over a million residents of Alabama, Mississippi, and other southern states said that they were South Americans.) Every time "Hispanic" is used in any Census table, a proviso is added that "Hispanics can be of any race." Even languace is not a common factor, since more than 10% of California residents with Spanish surnames do not speak Spanish. Moreover, Brazilians, from the largest nation in Latin America, speak Portuguese, not Spanish.

If "Hispanic" is used to define a race in the Census for 2000, which seems likely, horrendous difficulties will arise. First, there are a minimum of three million black Hispanics in the U.S. (If you are from the Caribbean, have dark skin, and speak Spanish, you are, by default, a black Hispanic.) To refer to black Hispanics as African Americans might just add to the confusion. Then, too, Argentineans are primarily of white European ancestry. Because of the pervasiveness of mestizo influences, most Mexicans could be counted as American Indian if they were born in the U.S. Today, a mestizo blood line is a primary background factor among Hispanics, most Native Americans, and most people from South and Central America.

This conceptual quagmire is the reason that the Census employed Hispanic or non-Hispanic as the only category of "ethnic group," given that no one knows what an ethnic group is. Now it appears that the Census for 2000 may well say that "Hispanic," having been an "ethnic group," will become a "race"— an idea that resembles science fiction far more than science. Given that the racial/ethnic categories in the Census are a scientific and anthropolooical joke, why do we keep the categories at all? The answer is a deeply American irony: we need the categories in order to eliminate them.

Without knowing who our oppressed minorities are, how can we develop remedies so that they will no longer be oppressed? Thus many people can benefit from checking off Native American, because special scholarships are available. In fact, the 1990 Census count of more than two million Native Americans is a demographically impossible increase over the 1980 numbers. Clearly, some people decided to chance categories. (And almost five million respondents in 1990 said that they had Native American "heritage" even though they were not Native American. It is certainly possible that two million of these five million will seek to reclaim that heritage in the 2000 Census, doubling the number of Native Americans with no increase in births.) Whatever this is, it isn't science.

If a box labeled "multiracial"—meaning any racial/ethnic mixing backed by four or more generations—were added to the next Census, estimates are that 80% of blacks and a majority of Americans in general would check the box. Thus the current black population of 30 million could decline in 2000 to a Census count of three million. At that point, there would probably be no federal aid to the 114 "traditionally black colleges." Asian Americans, most of whom are now marrying nonAsians, and Native Americans, who are producing more children in mixed marriages than in marriages involving two Indian parents, could virtually disappear from the demographic landscape. Hispanics could either become the largest racial minority or they could disappear, depending, on how many of them think their ancestry is mixed and on how the notions of "Hispanic race" and "mixed" are defined.

Consider some of the mind-boggling possibilities. If a Chinese American marries a Mexican American, is that marriage "mixed" in the same sense as if a black person marries a white person? What if the Chinese American marries a Japanese American? And most important, what if the Brazilian American who does not speak Spanish marries the Mexican American who does? What if your great-grand mother entered into a multiracial marriage? Does that mixing still count today? And do we want to force the children of mixed marriages to choose between their mother's ancestry and their father's? With what results?

It is painfully clear that our use of racial/ethnic categories as official data for the federal government needs a major overhaul, as the information these categories provide has become a political reality with virtually no scientific or intellectual validity. Millions of dollars hang in the balance, of course. Black, Hispanic, and Native American tribal colleges could close. Students could lose scholarships. Affirmative action programs might be dealt a death blow. Even departments of African-American studies and other minority studies programs and departments could be at risk. If we really want children to be judged by the content of their character rather than the color of their skin, as Martin Luther King, Jr., proposed, how do we make that happen? Still, the irony of arguing that we need racial categories in order to eliminate them is akin to the irony of the statement from the Vietnam era, "We had to destroy the village in order to save it."

While race has always been at least partly a marker variable for poverty, it may be time to go directly to poverty and see about desegregating it. Seemingly, we have been far more successful at leveling the racial "playing field" than at leveling economic differences. While 20% of black households are not above the average income level for white households, which represents significant economic progress for minorities, the data early in 1995 indicated that some six million children in the U.S. under age 6 were still living below the poverty line. Consider the issue of relative deprivation. Is a child with dark skin more likely to be disadvantaged in terms of life chances than a child born into poverty? Today, the anwer is clearly no; poverty is a more pervasive index of social disadvantage than is minority status.

Clearly, racial and ethnic categories in the U.S. Census are whimsical, changeable, and unscientific. It is also clear that distinguishing such physical characteristics as skin color or nose and eye shape is "taught" to Americans at an early age as a way of judging other people and that those distinctions have been used by our government since the first Census in 1790. As more of us marry across racial and ethnic lines, such differences will become even more blurred and less useful. And this leads to questions as to why they could continue to be used by the Census.

# C. Japan's Invisible Minority

NICHOLAR D. KRISTOF

*In U.S. society, most members of racial and ethnic minority groups are easily identified by physical and/or cultural traits. But in other cultures, minorities are defined in sometimes subtle and unclear ways. This reading discusses one "invisible" minority-the burakumin or outcast. They make up an occupational minority group but otherwise are physically the same as other Japanese. Despite progress, they still suffer severe discrimination in Japanese society.*

A 23-year-old woman had just given birth to her first baby when she learned something devastating about her husband. He was secretly a burakumin, a descendant of outcasts. So the woman refused to touch her own baby. She returned to her parents' house and abandoned her husband and child forever.

That was a generation ago, in Nagano Prefecture in central Japan, and the incident underscores a legacy of discrimination in Japan that has parallels in the United States. Even today, there is no better way for young Japanese to give their parents heart palpitations than by suggesting a marriage to a burakumin, and most burakumin still live in segregated neighborhoods riven by crime, alcoholism and unemployment. Yet Japan is also remarkable for the progress it has made.

Today almost two-thirds of burakumin (pronounced boo-RAH-koomin) say in opinion polls that they have never encountered discrimination. About 73 percent now marry non-burakumin, and most dismiss the possibility that the Japanese police might treat burakumin unfairly.

The E-word-Eta, or "much filth," the traditional word for burakumin-has been banished from discourse, so that virtually no Japanese ever uses it.

"I haven't ever encountered discrimination myself," said Masuharu Okuda, a prosperous 53-year-old who was standing outside his dry-cleaning shop in a burakumin neighborhood in Kyoto.

Mr. Okuda proudly pointed to his daughter-in-law, a woman in her 20s who was busy ironing shirts in the shop. "My son married a girl from outside the neighborhood, and she moved in here with us," he said. "There've been no problems."

Yet Japan has not overcome its divide. For if the three million burakumin, amounting to a bit more than 2 percent of the population, are now rarely burdened by overt

*Excerpted from Nicholas D. Kristof, "Japan's Invisible Minority: Better Off Than in the Past, but Still Outcases," THE NEW YORK TIMES, NOVEMBER 30, 1995, P. 18.*

discrimination, they face the same problems as some minority groups in America: disproportionate poverty, high crime rates, low education levels, many single mothers, dependency on welfare benefits and resentment from a public that believes they are getting special help.

The issues are those that Americans associate with race; in Japan the burakumin are not a different race at all.

They are an occupational minority group rather than a racial one. Indistinguishable in appearance from other Japanese, they were discriminated against simply because they were the descendants of people whose jobs were considered ritually unclean, like butchering animals, tanning skins, making leather goods, digging graves and handling corpses.

A related group of outcasts, also ancestors of some of today's burakumin, were hinin, or nonpersons. They were given tasks like torturing suspects, crucifying Christians and sawing off the heads of criminals for public display.

Outcasts were legally barred from marrying outside their group or from living outside their slums. These slums were called buraku, or hamlets, and that remains the term for a burakumin neighborhood.

In Japan, the outcasts were formally emancipated in 1871, but for decades after that they were effectively barred from ordinary jobs or any life outside the slums. Some Japanese shopkeepers so loathed the burakumin that they would wash their coins upon being paid. Such behavior has vanished, but contempt still survives in some households.

A university-educated housewife in Tokyo was scandalized when asked if she would allow her daughter to marry a burakumin. "Never, never, never!" she said. "Even if she wanted, I could not allow it. They're dirty. And they're not really Japanese."

Yet attitudes are changing in most families. A housewife in Mie Prefecture noted that the best friend of her teen-age son is a burakumin, and she said this had been a problem until the death of her mother-in-law a couple of years ago.

"My mother-in-law was a very good woman, but she had a terrible prejudice," she said. "So I could never tell her where my son's friend lived, even though he visited us all the time. She would have been furious. She would have said things like, 'He can't be allowed in the house! He can't touch the plates we use!' "

Now the boy eats with the family often, and the mother says she does not know if her son even realizes that his friend is a burakumin.

Some Japanese say the reason that their country has made progress with the burakumin is not broad-mindedness, but rather the inability to figure out who is a burakumin.

Burakumin are not easily identifiable by their jobs, for only a few of them now work in traditional fields like leather-making. The other big clue to who is a burakumin-an address in a buraku-is also less useful now, because burakumin have been pouring out of their neighborhoods while other Japanese have been moving in.

The burakumin are also invisible because there is a virtual taboo on discussing the issue. Newspapers and television stations virtually never mention the word buraku, partly because buraku organizations have sometimes denounced publishers for insensitivity when they have written about buraku issues. "There've been arguments in which burakumin said some very tough things, and so people became afraid of us," Mr. Tatsumi said.

Most Japanese clam up in horror when the topic is broached, and so most young Japanese know far more about discrimination against blacks in America than about discrimination against burakumin in Japan.

Some junior high school students in the town of Omiya, where there are many buraku, looked puzzled when the topic of burakumin came up.

"Who are they?" a teen-age girl asked. "I've never heard of them." Even many burakumin students themselves find out only in their midteens that they are burakumin.

"Most parents don't tell their kids," said Masahiro Takino, a city administrator in Kobe. "They say, 'Don't wake a sleeping baby.' "

Mr. Takino, who is in his 40s, first learned that he was a burakumin in the third grade, when he went to visit a friend's house. The friend's mother told her son, loud enough for Mr. Takino to hear, never to play with a boy from a buraku.

Japanese corporations used to search the backgrounds of potential employees to make sure there was no trace of burakumin heritage. Parents hired private detectives to investigate the pedigrees of their children's boyfriends or girlfriends.

Such searches are becoming rare now. Strangers are now banned from looking at other people's family registration certificates, where past home addresses are recorded. Private detective agencies are barred in some areas from checking on family backgrounds.

In the 1980s, the buraku were immediately recognizable as slums: dilapidated hovels leaned over tiny alleys, open sewers carried waste water into the rivers, and old people blinded by contagious disease sat hopelessly in the open doorways.

Now that has all changed. A torrent of government investment has improved the buraku so they are no longer slums.

Yet average income for buraku families is still only about 60 percent of the national average, and social problems are proving to be far more persistent than discrimination. Buraku leaders acknowledge that alcoholism is a disproportionate problem in their communities. Poverty and alcohol, in turn, weaken the family in the buraku.

Social workers say crime is a disproportionate problem among young burakumin, but the issue is so sensitive that no Japanese scholars have conducted research on it. One rare statistical study, conducted by Americans in the 1960's, found that burakumin youths were three times as likely as non-buraku youths to be arrested for crimes.

One explanation is that young burakumin sometimes feel that they are outside the umbrella of middle-class society. Denied the benefits by society, they also spurn the responsibilities.

Another explanation, aside from high rates of poverty and unemployment, has to do with one of Japan's open secrets: burakumin and ethnic Koreans dominate the organized crime gangs known as the yakuza. More than three-quarters of the members of the Yamaguchi Gumi, Japan's biggest underworld organization, are said to be burakumin or ethnic Koreans.

Partly because burakumin are so invisible, and because mobility is breaking down the barriers that used to keep them apart, many Japanese believe that burakumin will become assimilated over the coming decades.

Yet, for now, the progress is only partial.

# Resource Page

## A. ASIAN-INDIAN AMERICANS

### Study Questions

• Who are the Asian-Indian Americans, and where did they come from?
• How large is this U.S. ethnic group, and where do they live?
• What are the social statuses and occupations of Asian-Indian Americans
• What pattern of race and ethnicity as described in Chapter 8 do Asian-Indians follow?

### Key Concepts

acculturation
Asian-Indians
immigraiton
first and second generations

### Additional Resources

• Bridet Allchin. *The Rise of Civilization in India andPakistan*. New York: Cambridge University Press, 1982. A basic book on India-Asia.
• George J. Borgas. *Friends or Strangers: The Impact of Immigrants on the U.S. Economy.* New York: Basic Books, 1990. An analysis of immigrant's impact.
•George Eaton Simpson and J. Milton Yinger. *Racial andEthnic Cultural Minorities*. 5th ed. New York: Plenum1985. An excellent summary of minority groups.

## B. WHAT SHOULD BE CALL PEOPLE

### Study Questions

• Why does the U.S. Census raise an important question about what we should call people?
• What is at stake in the struggle over the definition of race and ethnicity in the Census?
• Why does the author's article propose substituting poverty for race as an important Census category?

### Key Concepts

Hispanic
multiracial
U.S. Census

### Additional Resources

• William Alonso and Paul Staff. *The Politics of Numbers*. New York: Russell-Sage, 1987. An excellent treatment of the misuse of statistics.
•Cornell West. *Race Matters*. Boston: Beacon Press, 1993. A statement in favor of race.
• William Julius Wilson. *The Declining Significance of Race*. 2nd ed. Chicago: The University of Chicago Press, 1980. An excellent treatment of race's problems.

## C. JAPAN'S INVISIBLE MINORITY.

### Study Qeustions

• How do the Japanese identify the burakumin as members of a minority group?
• How has Japan tried to protect the burakumin, and what problems do they still face?
• Where do many members of the burakumin ultimately find employment?
• How do the experiences of the burakumin compare to those of U.S. minority groups?

### Key Concepts

Burakumin
Eta
occupational minority group

### Additional Resources

• George DeVos. *Japan's Invisible Race: Caste in Culture and Personality*. Berkeley, CA: University of California Press, 1966. A basic presentation
• Mikiso Hane. Peasants, *Rebels and Outcasts: The Underside of Modern Japan*. New York: Pantheon, 1982.
• Clyde V. Prestowitz. *Trading Places*. New York: Basic Books, 1989. An Ameican's impressions of Japanese society..

# A. Dimensions of Filial Piety in Korea

YU-TAIK SUNG

*In most societies throughout history, filial piety helped provide for people when they reached old age.  Typically, a strong family would provide respect and support for the elderly in return for their own piety through the years.  However, with modernization and industrialization, family structure has changed and the status of the elderly has slipped.  This reading explores filial piety and aging among the Korean elderly and shows how Confucianism and a strong family tradition have helped provide support and care the elderly.   Their view of the elderly is in sharp contrast to current U.S. attitudes.*

For centuries, the value of filial piety has greatly influenced parent care and the parent-child relationship of East -Asian peoples.  The traditional value is associated with respect and care for parents and the aged, and is reflected in the ritual and propriety of the Korean people.

In recent years, the forms of respect for the aged have been slowly changing.  This change seems due to the movement toward smaller families, the expansion of the female labor market, the geographic mobility of villagers, and the tendency of the young toward more individualistic life styles.  Accompanying these changes in Korea is a decrease of the number of adult children living with their elderly parents.  The multigenerational family was the arena for the practice of filial piety.  Hence, declining parent-child cohabitation indicates a critical change for elderly parents.  The trends have given rise to serious concerns over family-center parent care in Korea: thus, a renewed interest in the ideals and practices of filial piety among concerned gerontologists and policy makers is not surprising.

Filial piety is variously defined in the literature.  However, the conceptualization that appears to receive popular support is the view that filial piety is "to respect one's parents and to care for one's parents"-the two principles that have been handed down by word of mouth.  To better understand this classic value of filial piety, its dimensions should be identified.

In the traditional Confucian notion, the aged are people who must be respected.  Filial piety inherently entails a "respect-the-old" ideology.  Material good alone do not suffice.  Filial piety has to be imbued with respect and warmth. A core ideal of filial piety is the fulfillment of a child's obligation to his parents.  Koreans still make conscious efforts to stress the ideal and practice of filial piety.

*Excerpted from Kyu-taik Sung, "Measures and Dimensions of Filial Piety" THE GERONTOLOGIST, Vol. 32, No. 2, 1995, pp. 240-246.*

In the present day, stories of filial piety are being told in school and at home via parents, teachers, news media, and books.  The stories usually illustrate the meanings of filial piety in all its ramifications, including respect, repayment, and family harmony.  The child of filial piety is the object of praise.  The social process still goes on in most of the intact and functioning families in modern Korea, although in a less intensive manner than in the past.

The major goal of this study is to determine the major filial piety constructs underlying 13 measures of filial piety.  The sample consisted of adult children and students of predominantly middle-class families representative of the municipal administrative areas.  Ninety-seven percent of the sample lived with parents.  The mean age reported was 34 years.  It contained diverse occupations, including student, housewife, shopkeeper, and public official.

Of all the measures of filial piety, "love and affection for parent" was given the highest priority and importance.  It is noteworthy that love and affection for parent emerged as the reason for filially pious parent care most valued by modern Koreans.  In Korean culture, where free expression of love and affection has traditionally been discouraged, this is an encouraging sign of change.  Love and affection is critically important; it is the force which unites family members.  However, love in no way undercuts the fact that there is a distribution of rights and obligations within the family system.  A great deal of support provided to sick and dependent elderly members by children may reflect obligation and not necessarily affection.  In fact, the findings of my study suggest a conflicting or mixed relationship between obligation and affection.

The measure of least importance was property inheritance.  It may be that people place less value and importance on material reasons for parent care than they do on more value-oriented, normative reasons for the care.

The six outstanding categories of filial piety are affection, repayment/reciprocity, family harmony, respect for parents, obligation/responsibility and sacrifice for parents. Thus, filial piety should be reconceptualized as not only including respect and care but also other variables describing filially pious parent care and the moral aspects of the parent-child relationship. The six important variables identified constitute the qualitative aspects of parent care. They are the virtues which Koreans have traditionally cherished.

Emotional responses were differentiated from behavioral responses. The first dimension, behaviorally-oriented filial piety, was measured by sacrifice, responsibility, and repayment. The Korean ethic of parent care is grounded in sacrifice which transcends self-interest. In the process of parent care, caregiving children have to resolve their constant burden, frustration, fatigue, and difficulty in dealing with their parents' disabilities, as well as potential conflicting family obligations. The greatest debt a child owes his or her parent is life itself. Parents take care of their children from the moment they are born until they are mature enough to take care of themselves. Thus, parental love and affection toward their children are perpetual. Filial piety is, in part, a desire of children to repay what they owe their parents for all the benefits they have received. Thus, the essence of this first dimension might be summarized as "the intent to do things for the well-being of parents."

The second dimension, emotionally oriented filial piety, was measured by harmony, love and affection, and respect.

Since filial piety is practiced in the context of the family, making family relations harmonious takes on utmost importance. In Korean culture, where the basic structure of personality is relational, family members maintain very close and cohesive relations. The individual member is made into a function of the totality of the family, in which family harmony is emphasized over individual well-being. The close and cohesive kin ties of Koreans have important psychosocial functions as well, such as the pooling of family resources and providing emotional support for elderly parents and other family members.

The key factor is the family: the family is the context in which filial piety is practiced. Therefore, the family's willingness and ability to provide care are critical factors. An adult child's family orientation is also an important factor. A filial child upholds his responsibility to his family, harmonizes relations between generations, carries out the wishes of his father, worships ancestors, and visits the rural home for an extended family gathering.

Old and frail parents desire attention and exhaust the caregiving child's time and energy, just as do their young, defenseless, dependent children. How much adult children can cope with parent care roles may depend both on their behavioral and emotional adherence to filial piety. Therefore, both dimensions of filial piety need to be considered in assessing the extent to which adult children will care for their parents. The six variables identified in this study will be useful in constructing a measure of filial piety.

The findings in this study indicate that the tradition of filial piety persists. It is likely that Koreans will continue to retain the cultural tradition which has had valuable results in the provision of pious eldercare and the integration of the elderly with the family and society.

# B. Warrior Narratives in the Classroom

ELLEN JORDAN AND ANGELA COWAN

*Chapter 9 discusses the role of schools in teaching children gender roles, and points out that books and teacher attitudes still contain messages of gender inequality. However, in many places around the world, feminists are trying to redo curriculum and otherwise change the thinking and behavior of children. This reading discusses such an effort in some Australian schools where children are not allowed to learn "warrior narratives" that support a distorted sense of masculinity.*

This reading is based on weekly observations in a kindergarten classroom. We examine what happens in the early days of school when the children encounter the expectations of the school with their already established conceptions of gender. The early months of school are a period when a great deal of negotiating between the children's personal agendas and the teacher's expectations has to take place.

We focus on a particular contest, which, although never specifically stated, is central to the children's accommodations to school: little boys' determination to explore certain narratives of masculinity with which they are already familiar-guns, fighting, fast cars-and the teacher's attempts to outlaw their importation into the classroom setting. We argue that what occurs is a contest between two definitions of masculinity: what we have chosen to call "warrior narratives" and the discourses of civil society-rationality, responsibility, and decorum-that are the basis of school discipline.

By "warrior narratives," we mean narratives that assume that violence is legitimate and justified when it occurs within a struggle between good and evil. There is a tradition of such narratives, stretching from Hercules and Beowulf to Superman to Dirty Harry, where the male is depicted as the warrior, the knight-errant, the superhero, the good guy (usually called a "goody" by Australian children), often supported by brothers in arms, and always opposed to some evil figure, such as a monster, a giant, a villain, a criminal, or, very simply, in Australian parlance, a "baddy." There is also a connection, it is now often suggested, between these narratives and the activity that has come to epitomize the physical expression of masculinity in the modern era: sport. It is as sport that the physicality

*Excerpted from Ellen Jordan and Angela Cowan, "Warrior Narratives in the Kindergarten Classroom: Renegotiating the Social Contract." GENDER AND SOCIETY, December, 1995, pp. 727-737.*

and desire usually lived out in the private sphere are permitted a ritualized public presence. Even though the violence once characteristic of the warrior has, in civil society and as part of the social contract, become the prerogative of the state, it can still be re-enacted symbolically in countless sporting encounters. The mantle of the warrior is inherited by the sportsman.

The school discipline that seeks to outlaw these narratives is, we would suggest, very much a product of modernity. The school is seeking to introduce the children to the behavior appropriate to the civil society of the modern world. An accommodation does eventually take place, this article argues, through recognition of the split between the public and the private. The outcome, we will suggest, is that little boys learn that these narratives must be left behind in the private world of desire when they participate in the public world of reason.

The school where this study was conducted serves an old-established suburb in a country town in New South Wales, Australia. The children are predominantly Australian born and English speaking, but come from socioeconomic backgrounds ranging from professional to welfare recipient. We carried out this research in a classroom run by a teacher who is widely acknowledged as one of the finest and most successful kindergarten teachers in our region. The research method used was nonparticipant observation, the classic mode for the sociological study of children in schools.

In the first weeks of the children's school experience, the Doll Corner was the area where the most elaborate acting out of warrior narratives was observed. The Doll Corner in this classroom was a small room with a door with a glass panel opening off the main area. Its furnishings-stove, sink, dolls' cots, and so on-were an attempt at a literal re-creation of a domestic setting, revealing the school's definition of children's play as a preparation for adult life. It was an area where the acting out of "pretend games" was acceptable.

Much of the boys' play in the area was domestic. On the other hand, there were attempts from the beginning by some of the boys and one of the girls to use this area for nondomestic games and, in the case of the boys, for games based on warrior narratives, involving fighting, destruction, goodies, and baddies.

"The play started off quietly, Winston cuddled a teddy bear, then settled it in a bed. Just as Winston tucked in his bear, Mac snatched the teddy out of bed and swung it around his head in circles. "Don't hurt him, give him back," pleaded Winston, try ing vainly to retrieve the teddy. The two boys were circling the small table in the center of the room. As he ran, Mac started to karate chop the teddy on the arm, and then threw it on the floor and jumped on it. He then snatched up a plastic knife, "This is a sword. Ted is dead. They all are." He sliced the knife across the teddy's tummy, repeating the action on the bodies of two stuffed dogs. Winston grabbed the two dogs, and with a dog in each hand, staged a dog fight."

In this incident, there was some conflict between the narratives being invoked by Winston and those used by the other boys. For Winston, the stuffed toys were the weak whom he must protect knight-errant style. For the other boys, they could be set up as the baddies who it was legitimate for the hero to attack. Both were versions of a warrior narrative.

The gender differences in the use of these narratives has been noted by a number of observers. Whereas even the most timid, least physically aggressive boys-Winston in this study is typical-are drawn to identifying with the heroes of these narratives, girls show almost no interest in them at this early age. Warrior narrative, it would seem, have a powerful attraction for little boys, which they lack for little girls. Why and how this occurs remains unexplored in early childhood research. Those undertaking ethnographic research in preschools find the warrior narratives already in possession in these sites. Even though the cause may remain obscure, there can be little argument that in the English-speaking world for at least the last hundred years, boys have built these narratives into their conceptions of the masculine.

The school classroom, even one as committed to freedom and self-actualization as this, makes little provision for the enactment of these narratives. The classroom equipment invites children to play house, farm, and shop, to construct cities and roads, and to journey through them with toy cars, but there is not overt invitation to explore warrior narratives.

In the first few weeks of school, the little boys un-self-consciously set about redressing this omission. The method they used was what is known as bricolage-the transformation of objects from one use to another for symbolic purposes. The first site was the Doll Corner. Our records for the early weeks contain a number of examples of boys rejecting the usages ascribed to the various Doll Corner objects by the teacher and by the makers of equipment and assigning a different meaning to them. This became evident very early with their use of the toy baby carriages. For the girls, the baby carriages were just that, but for many of the boys they very quickly became surrogate cars. The boys transformed other objects into masculine appurtenances: knives and tongs became weapons, the dolls' beds became boats, and so on.

This mode of accommodation was rejected by the teacher, however, who practiced a gentle, but steady, discouragement of such bricolage. Even though the objects in this space are not really irons, beds, and cooking pots, she made strong efforts to assert their cultural meaning, instructing the children in the "proper" use of the equipment and attempting to control their behavior by questions like "Would you do that with a tea towel in your house?" "Cats never climb up on the benches in my house." It was thus impressed upon the children that warrior narratives were inappropriate in this space. Warrior narratives provoked what she considered inappro For the very first day, she began to establish a series of classroom rules that imposed constraints on violence or disruptive activity.

One of the outcomes of these rules was the virtual outlawing of a whole series of games that groups of children usually want to initiate when they are playing together, games of speed and body contact, of gross motor self-expression and skill. This prohibition affected both girls and boys and was justified by setting up a version of public and private spaces: The classroom was not the proper place for such activities, they "belong" in the playground. Therefore, in this classroom, as in many others, these games were in effect banned.

The warrior narratives, it would seem, went underground and became part of a "deviant" masculine subculture with the characteristic "secret" identity and hidden meanings. The boys were no longer seeking accommodation but practicing hidden resistance. The classroom, they were learning, was not a place where it was acceptable to explore their gender identity through fantasy.

# C. Sweden's Liberation Goes Only So Far

WENDY SLOANE

*Efforts to change the social status of women take place around the world. Many experts believe that the society that has made the greatest progress for women is the socially progressive country of Sweden. Here, most women have jobs and benefits that protect them when they decide to have children. This reading, though, documents many ongoing problems women face in Sweden, including job discrimination and a lack of child care. It also discusses the efforts of Swedish women to fight against lingering gender discrimination.*

Five years ago Cecillia Omo was just another optimistic student preparing to graduate from dental school and begin a career in one of Stockholm's many state-run clinics. Today Omo and her partner, now in private practice, run a booming business and make more money than their husbands.

"If I were a woman, I'd rather be a woman in Sweden," Omo says, taking a hurried break between patients. "We can do anything that men in other countries want to do. Women in Sweden have it the best in the world."

Sweden has long had a reputation for being among the most sexually-emancipated countries in the Western world. Both men and women here espouse such progressive views on gender that they would be considered radical in many other countries. Compared to women in many other countries, the typical Swedish woman has it all: a great career, 2.1 children, and a husband who is as willing to fry the bacon up in a pan as he is to bring it home.

Homemaking and baby-care classes have long been required school subjects for both boys and girls. Discrimination laws make it difficult for employers to hire or fire on the basis of gender, and liberal maternity and paternity leaves, along with subsidized quality day care, facilitate women combining career and family. Fifty percent of all government ministers and 41 percent of the parliament are women.

But despite such statistics, Swedish women still talk of gender-biased problems. While Swedish women in general seem happier with their lot than their counterparts around the world, they are still likely to complain of a "mommy track" and inequality in the workplace.

For instance, while 84 percent of Swedish women work, only 48 percent have full-time jobs. And women who work full time earn 80 percent of what men earn. While

*Excerpted from Wendy Sloane, "Sweden's Liberation Goes Only So Far," THE CHRISTIAN SCIENCE MONITOR, November 22, 1995, pp. 1, ff.*

the gains Swedish women have made are considerable, feminists note that they have come about only in recent years. And although the status quo is changing rapidly, some achievements seem more style than substance.

Still, a 1995 United Nations report measuring women's participation in political, economic, and professional activities gives Sweden the highest marks of 130 countries investigated. In a general index contrasting female literacy, life expectancy, and economic data comapred with men, Sweden came in first place with a score of 0.92 out of a possible 1. This is a country where women don't have to choose between having a job and having children," says Ebba Witt-Brattstrom, a well-known feminist, literature professor, and soon-to-be mother of four. We have state feminism."

Swedish feminism often begins at birth, when both mothers and fathers are encouraged to stay home with their infants until they are old enough to enroll in day care. All Swedish women are paid 80 percent of their salaries from the state if they take time off to be with their children. Also, the government pays allowances of 750 kruna (about $ 100) a month per child, regardless of family income, to encourage women to have children, until the child turns 18. Child support and alimony legislation is also generous in favor of mothers.

Since few men have have taken paternity leave in the past, a new law encouraging them to do so offers parents 90 percent of their income, instead of the usual 80 percent, for 90 days-if the father stays home with the child for at least one month.

Such a climate may be behind the country's having the highest birthrate in Europe: 2.1 children per woman of child-bearing age. Roughly 90 percent of all Swedish women become mothers, putting the country second only to Ireland, where Roman Catholicism encourages high birthrates. In Sweden, birth control is freely available and sex education in schools begins early. Abortions have been legal for more than 20 years.

On the whole, Swedish women often have their first child relatively late: when they are in their late 20s or early 30s. Russian art historian Margareta Tiliberg says she began thinking about becoming a mother just last year. "I've always done what I wanted to do. I've always followed my own wishes, and now I feel prepared to settle down without regretting that I should have done this or that," says Ms. Tfflberg, who has lived in Switzerland, Russia and Japan. "Now that I feel like a whole person, I feel I have something to give a child."

But the nuclear family here is not considered to be quite as important as it is in the United States. Sweden ranks high among countries where people choose to live together rather than get married. Hence the word "sambo," the Swedish equivalent of "significant other," which can be applied to a man or a woman and literally means "living together." In the '70s, nobody got married," says journalist Katarian Bjarvall, who has been living with sambo Mustafa, and his three-year-old daughter, Lara, on alternative weekends for two years. "But in the '80s, there was a reawakening of conservative values and traditions." Ms. Bjarvall says she would eventually like to get married and have children of her own.

Her ideas conflict with many among her mother's generation, who scorned the idea of matrimony. "They thought marriage was only stupid symbols and empty traditions," Bjarvall says. "They would say that it's love that counts, not the symbols." But for some, these symbols are gaining importance. "We could have lived together, but we wanted to confirm that we'd try to stay together for the rest of our lives," says technical writer Eva Solum, who married sambo Mats in August, nine months after the birth of son Martin.

Many women in Sweden still complain of workplace discrimination. Women rarely fill top academic and corporate positions; only 7 percent of university professors are women. And low-paid, traditionally female jobs, such as teachers and nurses, are still filled largely by women.

The workplace gap between the sexes is widening, many say. Some women are reluctant to take full advantage of maternity leaves, saying they return to work only to find they have been passed over for promotion or missed vital training, which their employers refuse to make available later upon their return. "You often feel you are caught in the classical women's trap, when you are suffer-

ing from a bad conscience whatever you do," says Ms. Solum, who has been working only part-time since Martin was born. "You're either abandoning your child or you're abandoning your career."

"There is a special Swedish blend of emancipation," say Professor Witt-Brattstrom, who specializes in Nordi women authors at Stockhom University. "There has been an unwritten contract where the stronger sex says to the weaker sex, you can have a job as long as you stay below us. You can be my secretary, but I don't want you to be my boss."

This was demonstrated most colorfully in the early 1990s, when the conservative government was in power. As the number of women in politics had dropped considerably, a group of prominent feminists, including Witt-Brattstrom, formed a group to lobby for expanded female representation. Jokingly calling themselves the "Support Stockings," the group rapidly gained popularity. On the eve of last year's parliamentary elections, a poll indicated that the group would gain 43 percent of the vote if it formed a political party. The liberal Social Democrats, who would later win the elections, panicked.

Prime Minister Carlsson met with Witt-Brattstrom and another leader of the group and offered them a deal: if the Stockings refrained from forming a political party, he promised that 50 percent of his government would be female. The result, while strikingly progressive for other European countries, was disappointing to these women.

"Only some of the [female] ministers have power, like the deputy prime minister," says Witt-Brattstrom, who is still pushing for greater representation. "Most have low ministerial positions with tiny budgets.""Still," she says, "there is hope. While Sweden is far from perfect, the country has come a long way in the last few years."
She uses her husband, Horace Engdahl, as an example. It took half a decade before he turned in a sensitive '90s guy." An art critic with *Dagens Nyheter*, Sweden's largest morning newspaper, Mr. Engdahl is the first to admit he was a classic "male chauvinist pig" when the two first met.

"In my own family we didn't even carry our plates to the kitchen ourselves," he recalls with a hint of embarrassment, sitting in his spotless kitchen in Stockholm's fashionable Old Town after watching two hours of cartoons with his two youngest sons.

"It took Ebba five years to train me," he says, "I was disgusting in the beginning".

# Resource Page

## A. DIMENSIONS OF FILIAL PIETY IN KOREA

### Study Questions

• What is filial piety, and how is it supported by traditional Korean culture and religion?
• In what specific ways do families with strong beliefs in filial piety support the elderly?
• How does filial piety in Korea compare to the treatment of the elderly in the U.S.?

### Key Concepts

child-parent relationship
Confùcianism
filial piety
relational personality

### Additional Resources

• E. B. Palmore and D. Maeda. *The Honorable Elders Revisited.* Durham, NC: Duke University Press, 1985. A general discussion of the aged.
• Alvin L. Schorr. *Filial Responsibility in the Modern American Family.* Washington, DC
Government Printing Office, 1960. A basic study of family relationships and how they have changed.
• S.E. Solberg. *The Land and People of Korea.* Philadelphia: Lippincott, 1973. A look at Korean culture

## B. WARRIOR NARRATIVES IN THE CLASSROOM

### Study Questions

• What did the authors study, and what research issues were they exploring?
• What is a warrior narrative, and how does it express the traditional masculine gender role?
• How did the school try to relegate the warrior narratives in the private area of young boy's lives?
• How does this experience of children illustrate a modern practice ofseparating public and private spheres?

### Key Concepts

accomodation
bricolage
warrior narrative

### Additional Resources

• Raphaela Best.. *We've All Got Scars: What Boys and Girls Learn in Elementary School.*Bloomingon: Indiana University Press, 1983. A good summary of school experiences .
• James A. Doyle. *The Male Experience.* Dubuque, IA: William C. Brown, 1983. A basic text on the male gender.
• Linda L. Lindsey. *Gender Roles: A Sociological Perspective.* Englewood Cliffs, NJ: Prentice-Hall, 1990. A good treatment of gender roles.

## C. SWEDEN'S LIBERATION GOES ONLY SO FAR

### Study Questions

• Why do some women feel that "women in Sweden have it the best in the world"?
• What specific forms of discrimination do Swedish women still experience?
• How does the "women's liberation movement" in Sweden compate to similar efforts in the U.S.?

### Key Concepts

gender equality
mommy track
sambo
the Support Stockings

### Additional Resources

• Carolyn T. Adams. *Women at Work: Public Policies in the U.S., Sweden, and China.* New York: Longman, 1980. A look at three societies.
• Wendy Kaminar. *A Fearful Freedom.* Boston: Addison-Wesley, 1990. The U.S.'s best feminist writer presents comments on the current issues in the women's movement.
• Miriam Schneir (ed). *Feminism in Our Time.* New York: Vintage Boosk, 1994. Good essays on the status of women.

# A. Family Life in a Puerto Rican Community

*MAURA I. TRORO-MORN*

*Although millions of families have immigrated to the U.S. during the 1980s and 1990s, another period of intense movement took place during the late 1950s and 1960s. This migration involved people moving from Puerto Rico and the rural South to cities of the North, and established a pattern of immigration driven by economic forces. This reading reports on this early movement through a set of interviews conducted in Chicago's Puerto Rican community. The author discovered that economic changes caused families to move, and most families stayed together despite wrenching changes.*

From March 1989 to July 1990, I interviewed women in the Puerto Rican community of Chicago, which covers the areas of West Town, Humboldt Park and Logan Square. I participated in community activities and attended cultural events. These activities allowed me to meet the women of the community and, through informal snowball sampling techniques, to select interviewees. The interviews took place in the homes of the informants and lasted between one to three hours. Interviews were conducted in Spanish. The interview questions were organized around a series of themes, ranging from their migration history to family, work, and community experiences.

The sample of married women consisted of 17 informants. Eleven were mostly working class, with little education, who came to Chicago in the early 1950s and 1960s. Generally, at the time of migration, they were married-or were soon to be married-and most had children. The six professional and educated women in the sample had all migrated in the late 1960s and had over 14 years of education at the time of their move.

The most significant movement of Puerto Ricans to the United States took place at the end of World War II. In the late 1940s, the impact of U.S. investment and modernization of the economy transformed Puerto Rico from a predominantly agricultural to an industrial one. These changes in Puerto Rico's economy had profound consequences for Puerto Rican families. The development model was unable to create enough jobs, and working-class Puerto Ricans began to leave the island, heading for familiar place like New York City and new places like Chicago. News about jobs spread quickly throughout the island, as informal networks of family members, friends, and relatives told people of opportunities and helped families migrate.

My interviews suggest that working-class women

*Excerpted from Maura I. Troro-Morn, "Gender, Class, Family, and Migration: Puerto Rican Women in Chicago," GENDER AND SOCIETY, December, 1995, pp. 712 ff.*

and their families used migration as a strategy for dealing with economic problems. Married working-class women, in particular, talked about migration as a family project. For them, migration took place in stages. Husbands moved first, secured employment and housing arrangements, and then sent for the rest of the family. Even single men frequently left their future brides in Puerto Rico, returning to the island to get married as their employment and economic resources permitted. Some came as brides-to-be, as they joined their future husbands in Chicago. For example, Rosie's mother came to Indiana in order to join her husband working in the steel mills. He had been recruited earlier, along with other workers in Puerto Rico. Once at the mills in Indiana, these men often found better jobs and moved on. They went back to Puerto Rico, got married, and returned to Indiana. Others arranged for the future brides to join them in Chicago.

Married working-class women left the island to be with their husbands and families, even though some reported to have been working before leaving. Lucy and Luz were working in apparel factories in Puerto Rico when their unemployed husbands decided to move. Economic opportunities seemed better for their husbands in the United States and they both quit their jobs to move. For others, like Teresa and Agnes, both husband and wife were looking for work, when news about job opportunities came via relatives visiting the island. Agnes also came with her husband in the 1970s after a cousin who was visiting from Chicago convinced them that there were better job opportunities for both of them.

Working-class women also talked about the struggles over the decision to move. Fear of the unknown bothered Lucy. In addition, with a baby in her arms and pregnant with a second child, Lucy did not have anyone to help her in Chicago, but accompanied by her sister and her youngest child, Lucy followed her husband. Shortly after her migration, Lucy's mother and her sister-in-law arrived to care for the children while Lucy worked.

Victoria's story is somewhat similar. She was living in her hometown of Ponce when she fell in love with the son of a family visiting from Chicago. She became pregnant and, in keeping with Puerto Rican culture, she was forced to marry him. Without consulting with Victoria, the young man's parents sent him a ticket so that he could return to Illinois. Once in Chicago, he expected she would follow. The emotional and cultural shock was very strong. When her second child was to be born, Victoria was so intimidated by the city that she asked her mother to send a plane ticket so that she might go back to Puerto Rico. Within less that a year, she had returned. Eventually her husband joined her also, but he was not happy. So he began to disappear and neglect his responsibilities as a father. In one of his escapades, he went back to Chicago. Once again, he sent for her. Victoria had changed; as a married women who followed her husband to Chicago, she began to develop her own agenda and used migration as a way for realization.

In contrast to working-class migrants, moving was a joint family project for married middle-class women. In addition, the language this group used to describe the move differed from that of the working-class married women. Middle-class women came with their husbands and had an agenda of their own. Aurea met her husband while attending the University of Puerto Rico. Initially, the couple moved from San Juan to Boston to enable her husband to take a university position. In 1971, a new job opportunity brought them to Chicago. In fact, Aurea talked about moving as a mutual arrangement between her and her husband. She saw the move to Chicago as an opportunity to join community and political struggles. Shortly after arriving in the city, they bought a house-something that took years for working-class families to accomplish.

Brunilda had just completed her bachelor's degree and was working as a field researcher for the University of Puerto Rico when she was asked to work with a group of American scholars who came to Puerto Rico to conduct research in the 1970s. The researchers were very pleased with her work and offered her a position if she would relocate to Chicago. They promised they would help her to make the transition. She had just been married when the job offer came, and she felt that was a big problem:

"My husband did not want to come, he said that he did not know English. He just did not want to come. I told him that there were no doubts in my mind as to what that job meant for me. It was a great opportunity, and I was not going to let it go. If he did not want to come, then I guess that was it, I knew I was coming with him or without him."

In this case the roles changed. It was the husband who was asked to follow his wife; initially he resisted, but the job meant so much to Brunilda that she was willing to sacrifice her marriage. Brunilda, therefore, moved with a professional rather than a family network.

Vilma had moved from San Juan to Wisconsin to go to graduate school. While in Madison, she met her future husband and they moved in together. They had completed their degrees when he was offered a job in Chicago. In 1986, they both relocated to Chicago. Vilma described her move:

"I was very traditional in terms that I had just finished my masters and was looking for a job when my live-in boyfriend got a job offer in Chicago. I followed him to Chicago, but I came not only for him, but also knowing that in Madison there was no professional future for me."

As my interviews suggest, both working-class and middle-class Puerto Rican women found themselves migrating as part of a family migration. Married working-class women came to support their husbands and be with their families. In other words, their roles as mothers and wives compelled them to migrate. The narratives suggest that some women struggled over the decision to move. In contrast, educated married middle-class women were less encumbered by such relations of authority. They shared in the decision making and were less dependent on other family members to make the move.

# B. The Stern Mother and the Kind Father

LI ZHAI

*In many cultures throughout history the most typical family pattern featured a strong father and a supportive mother. The father would play an instrumental role designed to hunt or gather food, and the mother would nurture the children. But radical social changes in many cultures, including the U.S., has led to a reversal of these roles. This reading reports on a new family pattern in China, where the father plays the kind and nurturing role with the children, and the mother, who both works and takes care of the house, becomes a stern figure.*

The stern father and kind mother has always been the traditional image of parents in a Chinese family. But now, to many children, parents are playing different roles. The mother is strict and the father is kind and tolerant. The writer once asked six children aged four to six whom they liked best, mother or father. Four of them said they preferred their father. "Mom is the worst," said one boy, stamping his foot. Another said that both parents were equally kind. When asked why they like their fathers better than their mothers, they said that their fathers always hug them, take them to parks and buy toys and candies for them. Fathers smile when they talk. Unlike mothers, fathers never spank them. "Mom spanks me so hard, and she always gets angry with me," one of them said.

Zhi Yan, a 23-year-old kindergarten teacher said she believes what the children said. Working in a kindergarten attached to the ministry of Public Health, Zhi said she could see that mothers are generally stricter than fathers. It is mothers who force their children to take up various classes to study musical instruments, dancing, painting and foreign languages, whether their children like it or not.. Some children complain to their teachers or fathers, but they have to continue to study since their mothers are so determined. Mothers accompany their children to study in evening classes, sacrificing their own interests. In her kindergarten, Zhi said, many kids are overjoyed to see their fathers, not mothers, coming to take them home in the evening. Unlike mothers who forever ask them to behave and study, fathers often listen to their children, praising them for their cleverness and discussing plans for the weekend with them.

After visiting several families, the author found that "the kind father and strict mother" is really a common

*Reprinted from Li Zhai, "Role Reversal: The Kind Father and the Stern Mother," BEIJING REVIEW, January 17, 1994, p. 22.*

family phenomenon. Zhang Qin, a 28-year-old factory worker, admits that her son likes his father better. "It's unfair," she said. "I'm much more tired after a day's work than his father. All day I work hard and then come home to cook and do all the housework. I'm so exhausted that I have no patience to answer all the questions from my 4-year-old son, let alone tell him stories. I often feel inadequate because I have only a limited education and earn a low salary. I hope my son will have a good future. I often ask him to recite poems, and I'm so strict that I don't allow him to make mistakes. His father is an engineer at a design institute and his job is more flexible. He often takes the child out playing while I'm cooking. Sometimes he buys candies or small toys on their way home. Of course our son likes his father."

Which parent a child prefers depends on the particular situation of each family, according to a man whose wife is a manager of a hotel. "I'm not willing to be loaded down with housework and to look after the child. But I have no choice. Both her social status and income are higher than mine. And she is too busy. By the time my wife has gotten home at night the child has fallen asleep and is still sleeping when she goes to work the next morning. Even though she sometimes stays at home during the day, she is busy with her work and has no time to spend with the child. The child cannot receive love and warmth from her mother, so it is understandable she is closer to me."

To further support his point, the man said women in the old days were seen as kinder because the mother's duty was to look after her children and husband and do housework. Since they had no social or economic status, they had time to devote themselves wholly to the care of the family. It was natural that mothers were seen as kind.

While analyzing this family phenomenon, Professor Zhu Laoshi of the People's University of China said it is natural for parents to love their children and both are willing to spend more time with the kids. As mothers, women had been at the bottom of the social ladder for thousands of years, and they had a low position in their families, too. Although women's present social status is higher, the feudal concept that men are superior to women still exists. Some women unconsciously behave as "strong-willed woman" both at work and at home so as to gain a mental balance. Men, who are used to being in a superior position in society, often appear to be tolerant with children. Furthermore, most men are careless about family income and expenditure, so they will buy without hesitation whatever their children want.

Zhu added that in many families, fathers have received better educations than mothers and are more experienced in social interactions. Nowadays children are eager to learn things that their mothers find hard to teach. It is natural that they admire their fathers who can give them satisfactory answers to their manv questions. Zhu said the fact that many mothers are willing to let father spend more time with the children also contributes to the lack of mutual understanding between mothers and their children.

Moreover, many mothers still try to live up to the traditional expectations of children. They fail to adjust their thinking to a changing time during which family education should also be brought up to date. Fathers can generally keep a clear mind on how to educate children in these modern times. Meanwhile, they try to relieve the pressures on their children without offending their wives and keep the family going smoothly. It is no wonder that children like their fathers better.

# C. Global Family Decay

*SOCIETY MAGAZINE*

*The text thoroughly analyzes a wide number of changes underway in the U.S. family. Family change is also a global phenomenon. As the economy becomes internationalized and social pressures on families in many cultures intensifies, more divorce and out-of-wedlock births appear. This reading reports on new research documenting these changes in the family around the world and raises concerns about the future. The charts provided at the end of the reading are based on data gathered by the* Population Council *and clearly show the radical nature of these changes.*

Around the world, in rich and poor countries alike, the structure of family life is undergoing profound changes, a new analysis of research from numerous countries has concluded.

The idea that the family is a stable and cohesive unit in which father serves as economic provider and mother serves as emotional care giver is a myth," said Judith Bruce, an author of the study. "The reality is that trends like unwed motherhood, rising divorce rates, smaller households and the feminization of poverty are not unique to America, but are occurring worldwide." The report, "Families in Focus," was issued by the Population Council, an intenational nonprofit group based in New York that studies reproductive health. It analyzed a variety of existing demographic and household studies from dozens of countries worldwide.

These are among the major findings:
• Whether because of abandonment, separation, divorce or death of spouse, marriages are dissolving with increasing frequency. In many developed countries, divorce rates doubled between 1970 and 1990, and in less developed countries, about a quarter of first marriages end by the time women are in their 40's.
• Parents in their prime working years face growing burdens caring for children, who need to be supported through more years of education, and for their own parents, who are living longer into old age.
• Unwed motherhood is increasingly common virtually everywhere, reaching as many as a third of all births in Northern Europe, for example.
• Children in single-parent households-usually families with only a mother present-are much more likely to be poor than those who live with two parents, largely because of the loss of support from the absent fathers.

*Reprinted from Social Science and the Citizen, "Global Family Decay," SOCIETY, January-February, 1995, p. 5. Reprinted by permission. © 1995 by Transaction Publishers.*

• Even in households where fathers are present, mothers are carrying increasing economic responsibility for children.

The idea that families are changing in similar ways, even in very different cultures, should bring out new thinking on social policy, experts say, and in particular on the role government should play in supporting families.

The Population Council report says women tend to work longer hours than men, at home and on the job. In studies of 17 less developed countries, women's work hours exceeded men's by 30 percent. Data from 12 industrialized countries found that formally employed women worked about 20 percent longer hours than employed men.

Women's economic contributions also are becoming increasingly important. In Ghana, the report said, a third of households with children are maintained primarily by women. In the Philippines, women contribute about a third of households' cash income, but 55 percent of household support if the economic value of the women's activities at home, like gathering wood or growing food, is included.

In the United States, a Louis Harris survey released earlier this month found that nearly half of employed married women contribute half or more of their family's income.

One apparent exception to the general trends is Japan, where single-parent households and unwed motherhood have remained relatively rare.

The Population Council report, written by Judith Bruce, Cynthia B. Lloyd and Ann Leonard, found that while most countries have extensive data on women as mothers, there has been little research on men as fathers. But studies of parent-child interactions found no society in which fathers provided as much child care as mothers, and very few in which fathers had regular, close relationships with their young children.

And although fathers' incomes usually exceed

mothers' incomes, women usually contribute a larger proportion of their income to their household, while men keep more for their personal use.

Collecting child support is also difficult. The report says that among divorced fathers, three-quarters in Japan, almost two-thirds in Argentina, half in Malaysia and two-fifths in the United States do not pay child support.

The report emphasizes a need for new policies and programs to strengthen the father-child link-for example by allowing new fathers time off from their jobs, encouraging fathers to become involved in prenatal classes and familiarizing school-age boys with the demands of child care.

## Family Ties: The International Trend

DIVORCE RATES: Divorces per 100 marriages.

| | *Canda* | *Czechoslovaakia* | *Denmark* |
|---|---|---|---|

OUT-OF-WEDLOCK BIRTHS: As a percentage of all births in each country or region.

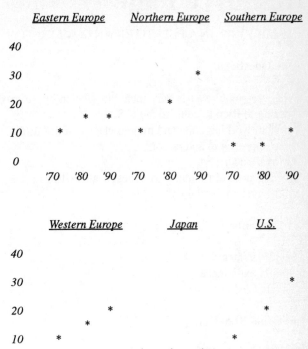

SOURCE: Population Council, "Families in Focus," 1994.

65

# Resource Page

## A. FAMILY LIFE IN A PUERTO RICAN COMMUNITY

### Study Questions

• What are some reasons why men and women chose to leave Puerto Rico to come to the U.S.?
• How did working-class and middle-class families differ in their approach to and reasons for migration?
• Overall, how did coming to Chicago affect life in the families the author studied?

### Key Concepts

economic strategy
migration experience
patriarchal society

### Additional Resources

• Oscar Lewis. *La Vida: A Puerto Rican Family in the Culture of Poverty*. New York: Random House, 1966. A class study of Puerto Rican migration.
• Earl Shorris. *Latinos: A Biography of the People*. New York: W. W. Norton, 1992. A good summary of latino people.
• Howard Zinn and D. Stanley Eitzen. *Diversity in American Families*. New York: HarperCollins, 1987. A good text on the family using an economic perspective.

## B. THE KIND FATHER AND THE STERN MOTHER

### Study Questions

• What are the usual roles of mother and father in traditional Chinese society?
• In what ways have those roles changed as China has industrialized and more women have gone to work?
• What kinds of problems in family life have these changes created?
• Have U.S. families undergone a similar transformation?

### Key Concepts

father role
mother role
role reversal

### Additional Resources

• William Goode. *The Family. 2nd ed.* Englewood Cliffs, NJ: Prentice-Hall, 1982. A basic outline.
• Christopher Lasch. *The True and Only Heaven.* New York: W. W. Norton, 1991. An excellent treatment of industrialization's impact on family life.
• Lorne Tepperman and Susannah J. Wilson. *Next of Kin.* Englewood Cliffs, NJ: Prentice-Hall, 1993. An international reader on changing families.

## C. GLOBAL FAMILY DECAY

### Study Questions

• To what extent has breakups of the family become a global phenomenon?
• What types of family breakups occur in many countries around the world?
• What are some of the causes of global family decay?

### Key Concepts

child support
divorce rates
feminization of poverty

### Additional Resources

• Alan C. Acock and Henry Demo. *Family Diversity and Well-Being*. Newbury Park, CA: Sage, 1994. A treatment of forces changing families in the U.S.
• Rae Lester Blumberg (ed.) *Gender, Family and the Economy*. Newbury Park, CA: Sage, 1991. An analysis of economic forces changing families.
• Mark Hutter. *The Changing Family: Comparative Perspectives*. New York: Macmillan, 1988. A good look at families in other cultures.

# A. What are Condoms Made of?

PAUL KLEBNIKOV

*Chapter 11 in the text discusses the country's concern with declining educational accomplishments. Although some commentators feel the problem is overstated, the facts suggest that U.S. children do less well in school than earlier generations. This reading's catchy title is designed to draw attention to this problem, especially when the U.S. school system is compared to countries like France, where students learn much more. It discovers some causes of poor performance in U.S. schools by analyzing what happens in French classrooms.*

In 1991 two international surveys measured the reading ability and math skills of 13- and 14- year-olds. Among the countries of North America and Europe, French kids came in second in reading (after Finland) and third in math (after Switzerland and Hungary).

Americans? We came in sixth in reading and tenth in math. Kids from such relatively poor countries as Ireland and Slovenia beat the daylights out of our 13-year-olds in math.

Yet the U.S. spends more per primary and secondary school student than any other country. We spend $6,010 per year on average; the French spend $4,600.

How do the French get so much more 3-R for the buck? In search of clues we visited two public high schools: Clarkstown High School South, outside of New York City, and Lycee Jean de La Fontaine in Paris.

Clarkston, with 1,400 students, is not one of those drug-infested, violence-prone high schools. It's in an affluent suburb of New York City, and its SAT scores are significantly higher than the national average; 92% of the kids go on to college.

The Clarkstown school is immaculate. Classrooms, with video equipment, brightly colored posters and potted plants, are pleasant, even cozy.

Now to France. The Lycee Jean de La Fontaine is a combination high school and junior high with 1,750 students. Like Clarkstown, it is considered good, but not top-notch.

At La Fontaine classes average 35, compared with Clarkstown's 21. Clarkstown boasts about 100 computers and a TV studio. La Fontaine has a dozen computers tucked away in a back room.

The rooms at La Fontaine are spartan-peeling

*Excerpted from Paul Klebnikov, "What are Condoms Made Of?" FORBES MAGAZINE, September 21, 1995, pp. 302-305. Reprinted with permission of FORBES Magazine.*

paint, rows of rickety wooden desks facing the blackboard. No one would argue that the peeling paint of La Fontaine accounts for the higher test scores of its students. So what does? The answer is almost too simple: a rigid curriculum and uncompromising standards.

Let's begin with standards. The French grading system is from 0 to 20, but hardly anyone ever scores a 20; 14 or 15 is thought to be very satisfactory. Grade inflation? American teachers often get criticized if they don't give out enough As.

For most Lycee students, high school ends with the baccalauriat-a grueling set of exams lasting 24 hours over the course of a week. Only 40% of Lycee students pass the exam.

American kids spend as much time in class as do French kids at La Fontaine: about 1,100 hours a year. The difference lies in how those hours are spent. The Americans spend as much as half the class time on touchy-feely stuff. The French stick to basics.

FORBES attended one such soft course at Clarkstown. This one is called "sex respect" part of the state- mandated Health curriculum. The classroom is filled with 15- and 16-year olds. The walls are hanging with posters and charts-eating disorders, sexually transmitted diseases, reasons for depression.

The topic of the day is sexual abstinence, but the talk is not about abstinence but about condoms. "Ladies and gentlemen," the teacher, Mr. Chiarello, tells the adolescents, "within a year you will no longer be able to call them rubbers. They're going to be made out of polyurethane. They'll be much thinner and more effective, like Saran Wrap."

Down the hall, FORBES sat in on another state-mandated course called Humankind. This is a replacement for the old civics course in twelfth grade. Instead of studying the Bill of Rights or the structure of American government, the kids discuss "issues" such as smoking, stress, alcoholism and homelessness. The teacher, Mr. Glotzer, leads a discussion on organized crime. The homework: a threepage magazine article on the Mafia. Then this class of 17-year-olds splits into six groups and draws pictures illustrating the point of the article.

Why pictures? "Sometimes kids are visual leaners," Mr. Glotzer tells FORBES.

There's no such straining at La Fontaine to make the curriculum "meaningful" or "accessible." About one-third of the kids study those least meaningful of all subjects, Latin or ancient Greek. Clarkstown has dropped these from the curriculum.

At La Fontaine we looked in on a seventh-grade French class. As Madame Thomazeau enters the room, the class stands up briskly to greet her. "Please be seated," she says.

The task today is to analyze the text of a medieval fable about a miser and an artist. Mme. Thomazeau grills her 12-year-olds relentlessly.

"How is the text organized? Where does the introduction end? Where is the moral? What words does the author use to switch our sympathies from one character to the other?" Mme. Thomazeau wastes no energy on fostering self-esteem. When the class is slow in answering, she thunders: "Half a year and you haven't learned anything!" Heads bend closer to notebooks, hands scribbling guiltily. More stick here than carrot.

"Speak up! State your argument!" the teacher glowers through her spectacles at one student who finally raises her hand. "Don't paraphrase the text. Synthesize!"

Let's now sit in with the 17-year olds in Ms. Gazzola's "Literature with a Difference" English class at Clarkstown. The students pick a short story that relates to their ethnic backgrounds. A girl of Indian descent picks "The Grass-Eaters," a short story from the subcontinent, but she doesn't analyze the story. Instead she talks about her feelings, about how the story reminds her of a visit to her family's native village. Quite interesting and gossipy, but the proceedings do nothing to advance the children's ability to read or write English.

"We used to teach a Judeo-Christian ethic," the teacher tells FORBES. "Now we're trying to work with different elements. We're trying to stress universality and commonality."

At the Lycee de La Fontaine, one-tenth of the students come from foreign lands, including Poland, Sri Lanka, Vietnam and Morocco. In this, French schools do not differ from many American schools. But here the foreign children must accommodate to France, not France to them, and there is no talk of "universality." The principal of La Fontaine, Yves Lancelin, declares: "We have no problem dealing with foreign cultures here. The students come here to learn French culture. And that's that."

That is not that at Clarkstown. FORBES dropped into Ms. Amster's ninth-grade Global Studies class. There's not much studying in it but a lot of discussion about current events. Today Amster is talking about the Philippines and how the U.S. allegedly supported dictator Ferdinand Marcos. She dwells on how many pairs of shoes Imelda Marcos owned.

"What's the standard of living like in the Philippines?" she then asks. "They're really poor," a student pipes up. "I heard they have people living in cardboard boxes and that many women work as maids."

The older generation among FORBES readers- could they understand the language-would recognize their own school days in a typical 1995 French schoolroom: a teacher lecturing to the class, lots of homework, emphasis on facts and formal logic, a right and wrong answer for almost everything.

Today in American schools the emphasis is less on facts and more on individual self-expression-which isn't all bad. U.S. schools encourage a more open view of the world. The French? "We have a rich enough culture that we do not need to look elsewhere," sniffs Raulin. That means no Shakespeare, no Steinbeck, no Dostovesky, no Gabriel Garcia Márquez-except in foreign language courses, which are notoriously bad in France.

Still, the much-vaunted "independent-mindedness" encouraged at American schools is often just sloppy thinking on the part of children who are spared rigorous standards. Glotzer acknowledges the problem, but says American society is to blame for the lazy thinking and low test scores. "Kids today are bombarded with such stimuli-Nintendo, movies, TV, video arcades, even the light shows at concerts-that you can't expect them to just sit and watch the teachers lecture," he says. "The kids don't want to learn that way and we can't make them learn that way."

For better or worse, the French system is less interested in making excuses for the children and more concerned with making demands upon them. "We have," says the French education bureaucrat Raulin, "very big ambitions for our *kids.*"

# B. The Jerusalem Syndrome

REBECCA LEE

*Sociology studies religion as a social phenomenon, and especially how religious groups of various kinds shape human behavior. Individuals can get caught up in religious movements, and encounter strong personal religious experiences. This reading is an example of the group's role in religion. It reports on the religious ferment found in Jerusalem and a large number of visitors who feel they are the "messiah" or a representative of God. These experiences occur often enough be called the Jerusalem Syndrome.*

A woman who believes she is the Virgin Mary enters the Old City through the Jaffa Gate. She is dressed in drab Western clothes, a nondescript skirt and blouse. An Arabian boy jumps out at her and gestures toward two cross, spitting camels on the sidewalk. "Would you like to ride, miss? Would you like to ride George Bush, or his wife, Michael Jackson?" Mary smiles and touches the boy on the head as she passes. She enters the long, snaking alleys of the Arab marketplace, walks serenely through, and shakes her head no to every treasure offered-a t-shirt depicting Yasser Arafat with an olive branch in his mouth, a vile of sand from the Dead Sea, a velvet rug depicting the Last Supper. She turns left into the Christian Quarter and then passes out of the sunlight into the perpetual cold and duskiness of the Church of the Holy Sepulchre, which is built on the hill where Jesus is believed to have been crucified. So many Christian sects lay claim to this church that the noise inside can be chillingly chaotic, all the competing services rising into a din of religious exhortation, a sound one might expect at the Tower of Babel. The geographic heart of Christendom in the summer of 1994 is deeply discordant, wild, dysfunctional.

Once inside the church, Mary veers right and ascends the stairs to the Room of Pity; it is lined with glass mosaics, one of which shows Jesus' body flung in various positions of distress. The room is dark; its windows are of milky glass, and faithful to the biblical metaphor, "We now see through a glass, darkly; but then face to face."

Mary pauses before the alter at Golgotha, said to be the exact place of crucifixion. She stands silent for a moment. Then suddenly she kneels, and as her knees strike the cool floor, her face distorts and she cries out, sharply. She lays her face on the floor and begins to sob desperately. Her day has begun.

*Excerpted from Rebecca Lee, "The Jerusalem Syndrome," THE ATLANTIC MONTHLY, May, 1995, pp. 24 ff. Reprinted with permission.*

Elizer Witztum, a cheerful man, is an expert on sadness. He is a professor of psychiatry at Beersheva Mental Health Center, specializing in despair, disorientation, and grief. "It is not effective to tell somebody she is not the Virgin," he says to me, referring to Mary. Witztum counsels people like Mary, who suffer from a psychological disorder colloquially called the Jerusalem Syndrome, an affliction peculiar to travelers to Jerusalem who snap under the historical and religious weight of the city and begin to believe that they themselves are the Messiah or the Virgin or King David or, more commonly, God or Satan. Many of these people have strikingly similar spiritual histories: a deeply religious childhood followed by an adolescent rebellion against their faith and an eventual falling away. Backsliders appear to be far more vulnerable to the syndrome, because their image of Jerusalem is sometimes drawn in a child's hand, unamended by adult reasoning.

The suffers are of two types-those who arrive in Jerusalem with a history of psychological or behavioral problems and those without any sign or record of past psychiatric problems. The former group compromises 82 percent of the suffers, according to Witztum. But those in the latter group, who are exhibiting what psychiatrists call the syndrome proper, are the more perplexing of the two types. Most believe for an average of five to seven days that they are some form of divinity; then they step back into the milder religious atmosphere of America or Europe as if nothing had happened. Of these, most are surprisingly responsive to therapy. Witztum described one such patient who spoke of the experience as being rather like intoxication. In the summer of 1986 he entered the Holy Sepulchre and was overcome by the feeling that he was Jesus. When he began sharing this conviction aloud with his tour group, he was taken to Kfar Shaul psychiatric hospital, where he was treated by the hospital's director, Yair Bar El. Within five days he was fine. He returned to his homeland, got married, and remains baffled about what happened. He is extraordinarily polite, as are many of the victims of the syndrome proper, most of whom don't rant but simply worry that they might be Jesus.

The former patient would like to return to Jerusalem for a visit but worries that the syndrome will strike again–as if Jerusalem were the problem. Witztum concurs. "This case was a reaction to a place, not a true psychosis," he says. In a new entry on the syndrome in the Encyclopedia Britannica, the question is asked, "Does Jerusalem's religious atmosphere actually induce psychiatric disturbance in the vulnerable visitor?" Though there is no definitive answer yet, Witztum believes that the "unique atmosphere" of Jerusalem together with the complexities of the human psyche may be more than some travelers can manage.

In order to explain the syndrome, Witztum differentiates between pilgrims and tourists. A tourist moves from the center of his existence, his home, to the periphery, in order to vacation. A pilgrim, however, moves from the periphery to the center of his world. Perhaps the best definition of "center" in this context was given by the religious historian Mircea Eliade, who wrote that the center is where the "axis mundi [the center axis of meaning] penetrates the earthly sphere."

Once a tiny hilltop fortification, Jerusalem has come to be the axis mundi for three of the world's major religions, where heaven descents to touch and bless the earth; Witztum calls the city "the umbilical cord of the world." Its hilltop location conferred a religious superiority on Jerusalem at a time when military and spiritual might were indistinguishable. "Their gods are gods of the hills," the ancients said of Jerusalem in the first chapter of Kings," so they were stronger than we." This inaccessibility also lent Jerusalem a rugged, evocative aura for pilgrims, an aura that persists to this day.

To live apart from one's center is, of course, psychologically disturbing, but the disorder that Witztum and Bar El have been elucidating over the past thirteen years is one that indicates how psychologically troubling it can be to enter or return to one's center. The center often cannot hold the weight of human longing. The place is either disappointing or overwhelming, and travelers frequently break down, to varying degrees. Witztum has said, "It is a problem of inner geography."

As for treatment, Bar El's methods are varied; he operates case by case, individual by individual, as seems necessary given the variety of patients he treats; a woman pregnant gain and again with God's child but unable to give birth until the entire world reforms; a Canadian Samson who weeps because nobody will believe him; a Jesus who calls the Israeli police to report unbelievers. Sometimes Bar El brings in family members to remind the patient of the real identity for which he or she is responsible.

"The most important thing, finally," Bar El says, as he walks me out of his office, "is to get them away from the stimulus. Once away from the City they are usually fine. " I walk downstairs and stand alone for a while in the shade of a pomegranate tree, staring out over the magnificent city–the stimulus–scattered over the Judean hills, its spires and domes rising and falling. It is so beautiful that for a moment I can imagine descending into it, abandoning my identity and taking on a more religious one, if only to belong inextricably to the city and its history, as a vein belongs to the body.

A small man with a beard joins me under the tree. I met him earlier in the day. He is a patient at Kfar Shaul. He said he was formerly a child psychologist at Yale University. Bar El could not introduce me to any of the messiahs, because of client privilege, so I ask the patient, "Do you know anybody who has the Jerusalem Syndrome?"

"What's that?" he says.

"When the identity of the land overwhelms the identity of the individual."

"Oh, that," he says. "Everybody in Jerusalem has that."

# Resource Page

## A. WHAT ARE CONDOMS MADE OF?

### Study Questions

• What is the major difference between the French and U.S. educational systems?
• How serious are the problems now facing the U.S.'s schools?
• Why have the U.S.'s educational standards declined so greatly?
• Why is the French educational system so much tougher than schools in the U.S.?
• Based on the readng and Chapter 11's discussion, how could the U.S. better its schools?

### Key Concepts

accessible curriculum
condoms
educational standards
individual self-expression
social values

### Additional Resources

• Jeanne Ballantine. *The Sociology of Education: A Systematic Analysis.* 2nd ed. Englewood Cliffs, NJ: Prentice Hall, 1989. A basic text on sociology and education.
• Allan Bloom. *The Closing of the American Mind: How Higher Education Has Failed Democracy and Impoverished the Souls of Today's Students.* New York: Simon & Schuster, 1987. A controversial book that documents a decline of standards in U.S. colleges.
• The National Commission on Excellence in Education. *A Nation at Risk: the Full Account.* Cambridge, MA: USA Research, 1984. The first study to document problems in the schools.
• U. S. Department of Education. *Schools That Work: Educating Disadvantaged Children.* Washington, DC: U.S. Government Printing Office, 1987. A good study.
• Philipee Aries. *Centuries of Childhood.* New York: Knopf, 1962. A classic statement about French children.

## B. THE JERUSALEM SYNDROME

### Study Questions

• According to the reading, what happens to many people when they visit Jerusalem?
• What social factors seem to promote the strong religious experiences in Jerusalem?
• Why have the psychological problems examined by visitors to Jerusalem been called "The Jerusalem Syndrome"?
• Where else do people experience similar religious upheavals?
• What social problems are created by the presence of strong and irrational religious beliefs?

### Key Concepts

Holy Sepulchre
psychological disorder
religion
religious exhortation
the Jerusalem syndrome

### Additional Resources

• Peter Berger. *The Sacred Canopy: Elements of a Sociological Theory of Religion.* New York: Doubleday Anchor, 1969. An excllent treatment of religion from a sociological perspective.
• Charles Lindholm. *Charisma.* Cambridge, MA: Basil Blackwell, 1990. A good account of spiritual qualities that draw people to religious leaders.
• Philip E. Hammond (ed). *The Sacred in a Secular Age: Toward Revision in the Scientific Study of Religion.* Berkeley, CA: University of California Press, 1985. Good essays on the conflict between science and extreme religious belief.
• Thomas Idinopulos. *Jerusalem Blessed: Jerusalem Cursed.* Chicago: I. R. Dee, 1991. A history of the religious struggle that is found in Jerusalem.
• Ninian Smart. *The World's Religions.* Englewood Cliffs, NJ: Prentice-Hall, 1989. A good background text.

# A. For a New Nationalism

### JOHN B. JUDIS AND MICHAEL LIND

*The new international economy and massive migration of persons around the world have weakened traditional ideas about nation and nationalism. In the U.S., many corporations and government officials seem more interested in international trade policies and politics than in the problems of U.S. citizens, many of whom have lost jobs or income. This reading calls for a new concept of nationalism that centers attention on all of the U.S.'s people. The authors argue that, to solve its problems, we need a new dedication to the U.S. and its institutions.*

In January, 1995, as the value of the Mexican peso plummeted, President Clinton, Majority Leader Bob Dole and House Speaker Newt Gingrich agreed to a U.S. Treasury plan guaranteeing $40 billion of new loans to the Mexican economy. The loans, it was hoped, would stop the peso's fall and also save the investments of American banks and mutual funds that had bought high-interest Mexican bonds after the passage of the North American Free Trade Agreement (NAFTA). As Congress began debating the deal, hundreds of CEOs and business lobbyists led by John W. Snow, the chairman of CSX and of the Business Roundtable, thronged Capitol Hill. With the President, the congressional leadership and the major corporations behind the bailout, approval by Congress seemed assured.

But it didn't happen. Democrats in the President's own party, many of whom had opposed NAFTA, and six rebellious Republican freshmen, inspired in part by Pat Buchanan's arguments against the bailout, rejected the deal. Within a week, the entire lobbying effort had collapsed. Clinton finally had to use his executive authority to guarantee the bailout, bypassing Congress and the constituents of the dissident congressmen.

The political uproar over the bailout demonstrated one of the best-kept secrets of American politics-the inadequacy of the ideological division between "liberals" and "conservatives" that we inherited from the cold war era. On this issue, the most hard-line conservatives were on the same side as liberals such as Ohio Representative Marcy Kaptur. Opposition to the bailout was neither a "left-wing" nor "right-wing," "liberal" nor "conservative" position. It illustrated a growing fissure that cuts across conventional left-right distinctions in American politics-the challenge to the globalism of the American establishment by nationalism and populism.

*Excerpted from John B. Judis and Michael Lind, "For a New Nationalism" THE NEW REPUBLIC, March 27, 1995, pp. 20-27.*

The opposition to the bailout was clearly populist; hard-working Americans were being called upon to protect the earnings of the rich. "We're not bailing out the people of Mexico," declared Representative Duncan Hunter, a California Republican. "This is a Wall Street bailout." The opposition was also nationalist. "I had two town meetings over the weekend," reported Texas Democrat Gene Green. "People were saying, 'We have a hard enough time in this country for small businesses to get loans. Why should we loan money to a foreign country?' "

This combination of nationalism and populism surfaced clearly in the 1986 congressional elections, then in the presidential primaries in 1988 and in the primaries and the general election in 1992. Nationalist and populist sentiments underlay the appeal of Ross Perot's "MADE IN THE U.S.A." campaign and energized Clinton's campaign against Bush. In both parties, nationalism and populism are embraced by the rank and file and rejected by the elites. Most conservative activists opposed NAFTA even though Republican politicians and think tanks supported it. Similarly, most of the Democratic Party's base has favored some degree of trade protection, but liberal opinion makers at the Brookings Institution, The Washington Post, The New York Times, the Democratic Leadership Council and The New Republic have joined elite conservatives in opposing any challenge to free-trade orthodoxy. We believe that in the coming years, the political debate will be increasingly shaped by populism and nationalism. The questsion will be what kind of populism and nationalism.

We have found that, among Washington's policy elite, describing oneself as a populist or a nationalist invites scorn and derision. Both terms, however, describe political traditions with roots deep in the American past. Populism was the name of a movement that lasted only from about 1886 to 1896, but populist themes emanate from the country's founding and have resonated through the twentieth century. Populism has been the classic movement of America's middle class-from its small farmers of the nineteenth century to its small businessmen and industrial workers of the twentieth. Populists saw society divided between "productive" workers in the broadest sense, which included farmers, artisans, businessmen and merchants, and the "idle" and "unproductive," which included coupon-clippers, vagrants and speculators. Like all political movements, populism has had its dark side. Under the populist banner, politicians have pushed everything from arcane monetary schemes to racial segregation to the expropriation of the rich. But what we would build upon is the conviction shared by populists and progressives that what government does must be judged by whether it benefits the great productive middle of our society.

We draw our version of American nationalism from Theodore Roosevelt's "new nationalism" "The American people," Roosevelt declared in 1910, "are right in demanding that New Nationalism, without which we cannot hope to deal with our new problems. The New Nationalism puts the national need above sectional or personal advantage."

America today faces a situation roughly analogous to the one Roosevelt and the progressives faced. Workers are not threatening to man the barricades against capitalists, but society is divided into mutually hostile camps: cities against suburbs, Northeast against Sunbelt, black against white. Particularly disturbing is the growing division along class lines-between a white overclass and an increasingly redundant and insecure working class in constant fear of tumbling into the underclass. The goal of a new nationalism today is to forestall these looming divisions in American society.

Our challenge is to replace these outworn ideologies of cold war globalism with a politics that more accurately reflects our new situation. For that, like Theodore Roosevelt and Herbert Croly, we propose a "new nationalism."

The first pillar of this new nationalism is economic nationalism. We believe that a strategy of limited protection for developing industries was critical to America's industrialization in the nineteenth century, to the rebuilding of Western Europe and Japan after World War II and to the emergence of East Asian capitalism today. We believe that a one-sided commitment to free trade was absolutely appropriate to mid-nineteenth century Britain and to post-

World War II America. But in the late twentieth century, the United States is in a much more ambiguous position, still possessing the world's largest market, but also highly vulnerable to foreign competition in many industries and incapable of competing in several, including areas of consumer electronics. This is not a situation in which a strategy of either rampant protection or one-sided free trade is appropriate. Instead, we advocate that the United States encourage free trade in the majority of goods and services. At the same time, it should reserve the right to protect industries such as machine tools and semiconductors that are important to the country's well-being and the right to pursue managed trade negotiations with countries such as Japan and China that have proved resistant to open trading.

Ultimately American economic policy must meet a single test: Does it, in the long run, tend to raise or depress the incomes of most Americans? A policy that tends to impoverish ordinary Americans is a failure, no matter what its alleged benefits are for U.S. corporations or for humanity as a whole. "I believe in shaping the ends of government to protect property as well as human welfare," Teddy Roosevelt told a Kansas audience in 1910. "Normally, and in the long run, the ends are the same; but whenever the alternative must be faced, I am for men and not for property." So are we.

The second pillar of today's new nationalism is national-interest realism in defense. We reject both indiscriminate retrenchment and indiscriminate commitment abroad. We favor a new defense policy tailored to promote concrete American security interests in the emerging multipolar world. from dominating these areas; our objective was not to achieve domination ourselves.

The third pillar of the new nationalism is a nation-uniting approach to social policy. We think the goal of social policy should be to reduce the growing disparity among economic classes. While we don't believe absolute equality is possible or desirable, we share the faith of populists and progressives that American democracy is incompatible with huge disparities in wealth and power. We also believe the goal of social policy should be to carry forward and complete the movement toward equal rights in our society by eliminating discrimination based on race, gender and sexual orientation. But this must be pursued with an understanding that we seek equality as citizens of the same nation.

# B. Private-Enterprise Communism

DWIGHT R. LEE

*Chapter 12 in the text points out that, only a decade ago, the world was divided into socialist and capitalist nations and economies. But with changes in Russia and East Europe, and the failures of socialist economic systems, new market forces are emerging. This reading describes one set of economic changes underway in Vietnam which has created a compination of private-enterprise and communist systems. The article's author points out that, despite total control by the Vietnam communist party, a free-enterprise market economy is developing.*

I recently went to Ho Chi Minh City, Vietnam, to lecture on the virtues of the private-enterprise system to an audience whose political allegiance is supposedly to communism. The reception to my comments was enthusiastic. Most Vietnamese want to live in a private-enterprise economy so they can enjoy the products that most poor people in the United States take for granted. But I was in Vietnam to learn as well as lecture. The most surprising thing I learned, given my uncompromising advocacy of private enterprise, was an appreciation for the political domination of Vietnam by the Communist Party and for the advantages the United States would realize from lifting its embargo against the Vietnamese economy.

I want to point out quickly that in addition to favoring private enterprise I also favor multiparty political democracy. But no matter where you want to go, you always have to start from where you are. And the fact is that political democracy does not exist in Vietnam. Opposing parties are not tolerated, and public criticism of the Communist Party is risky business, so the important question is: What is the best policy for moving Vietnam from its current autocratic regime to an open and democratic political process?

In considering this question one should recognize that while Vietnam's Communist government is hostile to those who want to practice political pluralism, it is increasingly tolerant of those who want to practice private enterprise. As Murray Hiebert noted recently in his Vietnam Notebook, "People seem free to do almost anything as long as they do not challenge the communists' hold on power." In response to economic collapse by a decade of socialist rule, the Vietnamese Communists began implemeting private-enterprise reforms in 1986. The offi-

*Excerpted from Dwight R. Lee, "Private-Enterprise Communism." Published by permission of Transaction Publishers from SOCIETY, January/February, 1995, pp. 64-67. Copyright © 1995 Transaction Publishers.*

cial political rhetoric is still Marxist-Leninist, but the economic reality is increasingly Adam Smith and Milton Friedman.

For many people, particularly those American loved ones still missing in action (MIA) from the Vietnam War, the type of economy Vietnam is moving toward may seem secondary to the fact that Vietnam's political regime remains closed, undemocratic, insensitive to our concern over basic human rights, as well as less than forthright about their knowledge about the remains or whereabouts of any Americans who might still be alive and held against their will. But the fastest path to an open and democratic government in Vietnam-and information about American MIAs-is the one that gives priority to private enterprise rather than political democracy.

The argument that communism in Vietnam can provide the quickest path to democracy depends crucially on the proposition that Communists can promote the prosperity that comes only from private enterprise. This proposition would have been ridiculed a few years ago. But the dramatic changes in the world's political and economic landscape in recent years suggest that the best hope Vietnam has for a vibrant private-enterprise economy lies in its current autocratic Communist regime.

The most dramatic change arises from the fact that socialist ideology is no longer powerful enough to blind Communist Party politicians to the most important economic lesson of our time: Market economies far outperform socialist economies at generating economic progress. No longer is it possible for socialist autocrats to keep their population unaware of how destitute they are in comparison to those in capitalist economies. And if maintaining political power requires embracing socialism in name but private enterprise in practice, few Comunist Party leaders have shown reluctance to so. Socialist autocrats are autocrats first and socialists last. China's powerful Communist patriarch Deng Xiaoping defended his "socialist" market reforms with the comment that he didn't care what a cat is called as long as it catches mice.

Certainly the Communist leaders in Vietnam elevated economic growth to top priority, even at the ideological cost of becoming private-enterprise "Communists." Vietnam's economy has a long way to go before it is a full-fledged private-enterprise system, but the movement toward the market is unmistakable. Since 1986, when the Vietnamese Communists began implementing their economic restructuring, Hanoi has abolished most trade restrictions, decontrolled export and import prices, allowed market forces to play a larger role in determining foreign exchange rates, and taken steps toward privatizing production activity.

Communist leaders may have the motivation to implement free-market reforms, but are they capable of doing so? Private enterprise has traditionally been associated with political democracy. It is natural to question whether economic freedom is compatible with political autocracy. But another dramatic change in the political and economic landscape has been the emergence of rapidly growing free-market economies under autocratic political regimes. These economically-successful regimes (concentrated in but not limited to Asia) provide evidence that economic lift-off through free market reform can be facilitated by autocratic political rule.

Why is an economy, based on private-enterprise capitalism the only type consistent with political freedom and democracy? Consider that the private-enterprise economy is a system of discipline and accountability that makes it possible for people to tolerate the freedom of others. Market prices, which are based on private property and free exchange, communicate information to all market participants on the values others place on goods and services and motivates the appropriate response to this information. Each supplier responds to the concerns of consumers by expanding output when those consumers communicate, through market prices, that the additional output is worth more than alternative products that could have been produced. Each consumer responds to the concerns of other consumers by purchasing more of a product only when he or she values the additional consumption more than other consumers communicate, through market prices, that it is worth to them.

The ability of private-enterprise freedom and prosperity to erode autocratic political power is certainly evident in Asia. Few would classify Taiwan and South Korea as ideal democracies, but it should not be overlooked how far they have moved toward democracy in a short time. As recently as the early 1980s, the populations of both countries were subject to a rather unforgiving martial law. The people of China, Singapore, and Vietnam are still denied political freedom, but personal freedom has expanded significantly in these countries as their economies have been liberalized.

No one is predicting that the Vietnamese Communist Party is about to fall or to voluntarily relinquish its political power, but there is no denying that the free market is beginning to undermine that power. According to Murray Hiebert, Hanoi Bureau Chief for the *Far Eastern Economic Review*, "Economic reforms are gradually eroding the [Vietnam Communist] party's flower. By abandoning farm cooperatives, encouraging private enterprise, and relaxing its restrictions on artists and writers, the party has weakened its grip over Vietnamese society." Hiebert quotes one party official who complained that "the party faces serious ideological erosion....The party bosses in the countryside are trying to accumulate land and the soils of the bosses are running private companies. The party has lost its heroic past."

The United States could have continued the attempt to pressure Vietnam to liberalize its political process with the economic embargo, but the Vietnamese Communists are notoriously tenacious in their resistance to external pressures for political reform. The most effective way for the United States to promote democracy in Vietnam is by taking advantage of the fact that the Communist regime in Vietnam is intent on promoting free-market prosperity. Opening up Vietnam to U.S. trade and investment will assist the Vietnamese Communists to achieve a vibrant private-enterprise economy that can only erode their political power from within.

Vietnamese communism has withstood the destructive assault of French and U.S. military power. What Vietnamese communism cannot long survive is the freedom and prosperity of private enterprise.

# Resource Page

## A. FOR A NEW NATIONALISM

### Study Questions

• Why do the political categories of conservative and liberal no longer describe the views of U.S. politics?
• In what ways has the U.S. become a divided country racially and economically?
• Why do the authors feel a new spirit of nationalism is needed in the U.S.?
• What are some principles of a new nationalism and why are they important?
• What could be the impact of a new nationalism on U.S. domestic and foreign policies?

### Key Concepts

multiculturalism
nationalism
nativism
populism
the progressives

### Additional Resources

• William Kennedy. *Preparing for the 21st Century*. New York: Random House, 1991. An excellent analysis of changes underway in the world.
• Michael Lind. *The Next American Nation*. New York: The Free Press, 1996. One of this reading's author's books on the American future.
• C. Wright Mills. *The Power Elite*. New York: Oxford University Press, 1956. A classic, and still very relevant.
• Francis Fox Piven and Richard A. Cloward. *Why Americans Don't Vote*. New York: Pantheon, 1988. A good analysis of why politics is not longer in touch with the problems of the people.
• Larry Sabato. *Power: Inside the World of Political Action Committees*. New York: Norton, 1984. A good view of a controversial area of U.S. politics.

## B. PRIVATE-ENTERPRISE COMMUNISM

### Study Questions

• What is the basic difference between priave-enterprise and communist economic systems?
• Why is the communist party of Vietnam allowing some free-enterprise activity?
• Why does free-enterprise economic activity promote political democracy?
• Why does Vietnam still have a long way to go before it becomes a totally free-enterprise economy?
• What has been the attitudes of the U.S. to changes in Vietnam society?

### Key Concepts

Communism
economic restructuring
political democracy
private enterprise
Vietnam

### Additional Resources

• Peter Berger. *The Capitalism Revolution: Fifty Propositions About Prosperity, Equality, and Liberty*. New York: Basic Books, 1986. An excellent analysis of capitalism.
• Robert Heilbroner. 21st Century Capitalism. Englewood Cliffs, NJ: Prentice-Hall, 1992. A leading economist analyzes powerful trends in the world economy.
• Karl Marx. *Selected Writings in Sociology and Social Philosophy*. New York: McGraw-Hill, 1964. A collection of Marx's most important writing.
• Michael E. Porter. *The Competitive Advantage of Nations*. New York: Free Press, 1990. A basic treatment of economic life.
• Nancy Wiegersma. *Reinventing Vietnam's Socialism: Doi Moi in Comparative Perspective*. Boulder, CO: Westview Press, 1993. Good background on Vietnam's economy.

# A. Western Bioethics on the Navajo Reservation

*JOSEPH A. CARRESE AND LORNA A. RHODES*

*The diversity of the U.S. population is encouraging many professionals, including college professors and social workers, to become more knowledgeable about other cultures and to adapt their ways of proceeding. This reading serves as an example of this trend. It shows the conflict that can arise between doctors try to provide care to residents of a Navajo reservation, especially the issues of bioethics, the patient's right to knowledge about his disease and self-determination.*

The United States is a pluralistic society, consisting of people from many different traditions and from diverse cultural backgrounds. Accordingly, not all patients share the values and moral perspectives of dominant society as currently reflected in mainstream Western biomedicine and bioethics. Surprisingly, little research has been done on the variability of patients' values and moral perspectives by community as compared with prevailing societal, biomedical, and bioethical views. Yet, as demonstrated by two recent studies, one comparing Mexican-American and Anglo-American attitudes toward autopsies, and the other comparing attitudes about end-of-life care among African Americans, Hispanics, and non-Hispanic whites, there are important differences to be appreciated. One of us practiced medicine on the Navajo Indian reservation in northeast Arizona between 1988 and 1992 and observed that Western biomedical and bioethical concepts and principles often conflicted with traditional Navajo values and ways of thinking. This study examined one such area of conflict: discussing "negative information" with Navajo patients. Examples of negative information include the disclosure of risk and "bad news."

In the culture of Western biomedicine and bioethics, the principles of autonomy and patient self-determination are centrally important. Consequently, explicit and direct discussion of negative information between health care providers and patients is the current standard of care. For example, informed consent requires disclosing the risks of medical treatments and truth telling requires disclosure of bad news. Physicians have been criticized for failing to meet these standards.

In traditional Navajo culture, it is held that thought and language have the power to shape reality and to control events. Discussing the potential complications of dia-

Excerpted from Joseph A. Carrese and Lorna A. Rhodes, "Western Bioethics on the Navajo Reservation," JOURNAL OF THE AMERICAN MEDICAL ASSOCIATION, September 13, 1995, pp. 826-829,

betes with a newly diagnosed Navajo patient may, in the view of the traditional patient, result in theoccurrence of such complications. As anthropologist Gary Witherspoon notes: "In the Navajo view of the world, language is not a mirror of reality, reality is a mirror of language." Restated, in the Navajo view, language does not merely describe reality, language shapes reality. For these reasons traditional Navajo patients may regard the discussion of negative information as potentially harmful.

In this study we were interested to learn how health care providers should approach the discussion of negative information with Navajo patients. Achieving a better understanding of the Navajo perspective on these issues might result in more culturally appropriate medical care for Navajo patients in Western hospitals and clinics. Finally, this inquiry provided the opportunity to consider the limitations of dominant Western bioethical perspectives.

The study was a focused ethnography. Ethnography is helpful in understanding the differences between various cultures and systems of meaning. Fieldwork was conducted between February 1993 and March 1994 on four trips to the Navajo Indian reservation, which is located primarily in northeast Arizona, but also includes portions of southern Utah and northwest New Mexico. The Navajo reservation is approximately 25,000 square miles, about the size of West Virginia; it is the largest Indian reservation in the United States."

Two sampling strategies were used in this study. First, purposeful or judgment sampling was used in the recruitment of several key informants, such as public health nurses, community health representatives, a Veterans Affairs representative, a social worker, and mental health workers. Judgment sampling was also used by the key informants, who were primarily responsible for the selection of study informants. Second, in a few cases informants themselves identified others who should be interviewed; this represents network or snowball sampling. These approaches generated a group of informants from different tribal clans and having different locations of residence and medical problems. Thirty-four Navajo informants were interviewed, 16 men and 18 women. The age range was 26 to 87 years, with a median of 58.5 years and a mean of 60 years. We deliberately included a subgroup of eight Navajo biomedical health care providers because they were in a unique position to comment on the traditional Navajo culture as well as the Western biomedical culture.

Transcript analysis identified several themes; only a portion of the findings will be presented here. First, we describe two themes that emerged from the open-ended interviews, followed by data regarding informants' opinions about advance care planning. Informants commented often that it was important to "think and speak in a positive way." This theme is encompassed by the Navajo phrases *hozhooji nitsihakees* and *hozhoojfi saad*. The literal translations are "think in the Beauty Way" and "talk in the Beauty Way." The prominence of these themes reflects the Navajo view that thought and language have the power to shape reality and control events. A public health nurse referred us to a woman who had resisted attending a prenatal clinic. In the woman's experience the risks of pregnancy were discussed at the clinic, a practice she found troubling. She made the following remarks: " I've always thought in a positive way, ever since I was young. And even when the doctors talked to me like that, I always thought way in the back of my mind: I'm not going to have a breech baby. I'm going to have a healthy baby and a real fast delivery with no complications, and that's what has happened."

This theme of thinking and speaking in a positive way often emerged when informants reflected on how doctors should communicate with patients; it reflects the Navajo view that health is maintained and restored through positive ritual language. A traditional diagnostician, commenting on how she counsels her own patients on matters of health and illness, said the following:

In order to think positive there are plants up in the mountains that can help you. Also there are prayers that can be done. You think in these good ways, and that will make you feel better and whatever has stricken you in the deadly manner will kind of fall apart with all these good things that you put in place of it.... The doctor may say, "You're not going to live," but I say, *"Hozhooji nitsihakees"*; that means "Think in the Beauty Way."

Informants made a related point of requesting that providers "avoid thinking or speaking in a negative way." This theme is approximated by the Navajo phrase, "Doo'djiniidah." The literal translation is "Don't talk that way!" Often this theme was expressed as informants recounted interactions with medical providers that upset them, the idea being that negative thoughts and words can result in harm. A middle-aged Navajo woman who is a nurse, speaking about how the risks of bypass surgery were explained to her father, said the following:

The surgeon told him that he may not wake up, that this is the risk of every surgery. For the surgeon it was very routine, but the way that my Dad received it, it was almost like a death sentence, and he never consented to the surgery.

Our study sought to understand the perspective of Navajo informants regarding the discussion of negative information. Two closely related themes emerged from the interviews. Informants explained that patients and health care providers should think and speak in a positive way and avoid thinking or speaking in a negative way. It is clear that these Navajo informants have their own way of thinking about and coping with issues related to safety and danger, health and sickness, and life and death. It is a way of thinking and using language that reflects the Navajo view that thought and language shape reality. Discussing negative information conflicts with the Navajo view of language and its relationship to reality and with our informants' expectation that communication between healers and patients embodies the concept of hozho.

One limitation of this study is that the findings reflect a more traditional perspective; the full range or diversity of Navajo views on these matters is not represented. Some Navajos who seek health care in Indian Health Service hospitals and clirdcs, particularly those who are more acculturated to mainstream American society, may be comfortable with and even expect frank discussion about the risks of medical treatment

This study further demonstrates that the concepts and principles of Western bioethics are not universally held. In our pluralistic society there are communities of patients who do not identify dominant values as their own, a fact that health care providers and institutions need to appreciate. A deeper understanding of patients' perspectives should follow, and this in turn should be used to inform clinical interactions, research and educational activities, and institutional policies.

# B. AIDS and the Social Body in Cuba

NANCY SCHEPER-HUGHES

*The AIDs epidemic has reached every corner of the world and challenges different countries to respond to this health crisis. The "social body" or the "community" of a country can respond in many ways, such as medical research, outreach programs and experimental drug therapies. Cuba's reaction, as described in this reading, is unique. It uses a public health model, where most citizens are tested for the AIDS virus and those detected with it are placed in quarantine.*

Cuba represents another sort of human and public health nightmare, through a nightmare of hyper-vigilant medical police and of over-observed and overdisciplined bodies: a nightmare of medical 'discipline' verging on 'punishment'. The contrast with Brazil (and with the United States and France) could not be more striking. Cuba is the only nation to have used the 'classic' public health tradition—routine testing, contact tracing with partner notification, close medical surveillance and partial isolation of all seropositive individuals-within a national program to contain the spread of the epidemic on the island. With only 927 cases of seropositivity [through May 1993], 187 persons with AIDS, and only 111 deaths overall in a population of more than 10.5 million, the Cuban AIDS program seems to be succeeding.

The success is even more impressive when one compares Cuba to its immediate neighbors in the Caribbean where the prevalence rates for AIDS are similar to, or greater than, the United States. Puerto Rico, with one third the population of Cuba, has over 8000 cases of AIDS, 208 of them pediatric cases. In Cuba only one child has died of AIDS, and only three more are carrying the virus. In New York City, with roughly the same population as Cuba, 43,000 people are currently sick with AIDS. In contrast to France and Brazil where thousands of citizens have been infected with contaminated blood supplies due to official indifference and public irresponsibility, only 9 Cubans have ever been infected through blood transfusion.

There were many factors contributing to the control of the AIDS epidemic independent of the Cuban public health program. Cuba is an island and has been both harrassed and (in the case of AIDS) protected by the U.S. embargo designed to isolate the country. Consequently, until recently, there has been little IV drug use on the island. Cuba's climate of socialist sexual puritanism led to

*Excerpted from Nancy Scheper-Hughes, "AIDS and the Social Body," SOCIAL SCIENCE AND MEDICINE, VOL. 39, NO. 7, 1994, PP. 991-1003.*

an early exodus of gay Cubans from the island. Meanwhile, the easy and universal access to abortion as primary means of birth control has been put into the service of AIDS control and most HIV positive pregnant women elect to abort rather than chance a pregnancy viewed as fraught with risk to themselves and to their unborn child.

Cuban health officials had advance warning of the epidemic and with Cuba's comprehensive health system already in place, officials were able to mobilize early and decisively. AIDS was never treated in Cuba (as it was in virtually all western democracies) as a "special case," one to be treated gingerly by public officials for fear of offending or stigmatizing high risk populations. Instead, it was viewed and treated as any other major threat to public health following a model of socialist rational planning that flies in the face of the global neo-liberal political spirit of the times.

The Cuban AIDS program has been sharply criticized throughout the West (and by the World Health Organization) for its violations of the privacy and liberty of scropositive people. Most of the criticism concerns the AIDS sanatorium. By contrast, there has been almost no attention to the equally severe Cuban policy of recommending routine abortion to all pregnant women who test seropositive. But Cuban health officials remain uncowed by the condemnation of their program. The proof, they say, is in the pudding: Cubans are not dying of AIDS. In fact, Cuba is one of the only countries where new cases are actually decreasing. The international community has replied that it is unimpressed with Cuban 'pragmatism'. And, in place of the old aphorism-the operation was a (technical) success, but the patient died-one hears it said that Cubans may not be dying of AIDS, but the operation is a (moral) failure.

Those international researchers who have actually visited the Cuban sanatoria and personally reviewed the Cuban medical records, the quality of medical care and the social services available to residents, return favorably impressed. Even as dogged a critique of the Cuban model as Jonathan Mann, former director of the WHO, AIDS program, noted his positive impression of patient care on the first page of the visitor register of the Havana sanatorium. But outside observers continue to judge the Cuban program an anachronism in the exquisitely civil libertarian climate of late 20th century.

In June 1991 and again in May 1993, I went to Cuba to explore the controversial program from the perspective of critical and feminist medical anthropology. After meeting with Dr. Hector Terry, until recently the Vice-Minister of MINSAP, the Cuban Ministry of Public Health, I received permission to visit the sanatorium of Santiago de las Vegas, on the outskirts of Havana. In between these two visits I invited the director of the AIDS sanatorium, Dr. Jorge Perez, to the University of California, Berkeley, in September 1992 and, in December 1992 I cosponsored the visit to the Bay area of two sanatorium patients, Dr. Juan Carlos, and his partner, the late Raul Llanos, both AIDS activists and AIDS prevention educators.

At the expense of being labeled an AIDS heretic, I remain impressed with the Cuban success against AIDS. Consequently, the full AIDS tragedy that one finds in nearby Haiti and Miami, or in Brazil, where the epidemic readily spread from one "risk group" to another—as it certainly would have in Cuba where a pattern of bisexual transmission between gay and heterosexual partners has been clearly identified was averted. This public health accomplishment, generally lost in the individual rights debates, is remarkable.

The Cuban AIDS policy evolved through various stages of trial and error from 1983 to the present. When Cuban officials learned of the AIDS epidemic, following a Pan American Health Organization meeting in 1983, they established a national AIDS program. The first initiative was to ban the importation of blood derivatives from countries where AIDS already existed and where blood banks were commercially owned (in the Cuban vernacular, "capitalist blood"), thus eliminating from the start a major source of infection. When the first commercial tests for anti-HIV antibodies became available on the international market in 1985, the Cuban government began a program of testing all Cubans who had been out of the country since 1981. In the first population of identified seropositive persons were a large number of Cuban internationalists returning from combat duty in Africa. By June of 1986 AIDS testing was extended to include all blood donors and all those whose work exposed them to risk by extensive travel, such as tourist and resort and airline workers, fishermen and merchant marine.

A cornerstone of the Cuban AIDS program was the creation in 1985 of a special epidemiological group to trace and to test on a regular (and repeated) basis the sexual partners of all seropositive persons. For each seropositive person there is a confidential sexual contact "tree" that traces the spread of the disease through various sexual partners, all of whom are eventually contacted and screened.

Beginning in 1986 and continuing to today, although with significant modifications, all Cubans who test positive for the AIDS virus are expected to live, more or less permanently at one of 12 AIDS residential communities in Cuba. Critics in the west call them "quarantine," if they are delicate, or "concentration or prison camps," if they are not. The point of the sanatorium, Cuban officers argue was never guarantine. The purpose of the sanatorium is aggressive medical treatment, and experimental testing of new drugs, and a epidemiological surveillance. A sanatorium is by nature a dual institution, an odd blend of care and coercion. The sanatorium serves two masters and the physician is a kind of double agent. But in the face of an epidemic the doctor has two patients: the infected person who needs compassion and the community (the social body) which need protection from a deadly disease. The Cuban program is able to balance these competing needs.

I returned from Cuba each time with many contradictory impressions and with many questions. When is 'good medicine' altogether too much medicine and too bitter a pill to swallow? Under what conditions is a medical policy as restrictive of individual human rights as Cuba's ethically warranted? There is abundant positive epidemiological evidence in terms of the longevity of AIDS sanatoria residents and in the low incidence of new seropositive cases. That the Cubans may have accomplished this by means of the very same methods that were rejected in the United States as violations of individual rights gives reason to pause. Since we have been far less successful in combating the AIDS epidemic, facile ideological criticisms of the Cuban program seem out of place. But if the same salutary effects could have been accomplished in Cuba short of imposing the sanatorium system, then Cuba has the devil to pay its violated scropositive citizens. Appropriate restitution can never be made.

# Resource Page

## A. WESTERN BIOETHICS ON THE NAVAJO RESERVATION

### Study Questions

• What are bioethics and how do they influence medical practice?
• How do the Navajo think differently about life and reality?
• In what ways do the Navajo's traditional ways of thinking come in conflict with Western bioethics?
• How might doctors be more sensitive to Navajo culture regarding informed consent and self-determination?
• What are your own views about the bioethical issue raised in the reading?

### Key Concepts

bioethics
informants
language
Navajo Indians
patient self-determination

### Additional Resources

• Michael Agar. *Speaking of Ethnography*. Newbury Park, CA: Sage, 1986. A basic text on the study of cultures, by an expert.
• T. M. Johnson and C. E. Sargent (eds). *Medical Anthropology: Contemporary Theory and Method*. New York: Praeger, 1990. A basic text on the anthropological study of medicine.
• A. Kleinman. *The Illness Narratives: Suffering, Healing, and the Human Condition*. New York: Basic Books, 1988. A good book on different experiences with pain.
• R. F. Locke. *The Book of the Navajo*. Los Angeles, CA: Mankind Publishing, 1976. A good treatment of Navajo culture.
• Anthony P. Polednak. *Racial and Ethnic Differences in Disease*. New York: Oxford University Press, 1989. A good treatment of disease in other cultures.

## B. AIDS AND THE SOCIAL BODY IN CUBA

### Study Questions

• Why does AIDS/HIV pose a health risk for the "social body" in many countries of the world?
• What is the public health model used by Cuba to deal with AIDS?
• How does the use of sanatoriums different from the U.S. policy regarding persons infected with the HIV virus?
• What are the pros and cons of the Cuban model of treating the AIDS epidemic, according to the author?
• What parts of the Cuban approach to AIDS could be used in the U.S.?

### Key Concepts

AIDS/HIV
Cuba
quarantine
sanatoriums
social body

### Additional Resources

• Inge B. Corless and Mary Pittman-Lindman. *AIDS: Principles, Practices, and Politics*. New York: Hemisphere, 1987. A basic book on the AIDS problem.
• Dorothy Nelkin, David P. Willis, and Scott V. Parris (eds). *A Disease of Society: Cultural and Institutional Responses to AIDS*. Cambridge, UK: Cambridge University Press, 1991. A good treatment of several responses to AIDS.
• Lynn Payer. *Medicine and Culture*. New York: Holt, 1988. A good book on the impact of culture on the definition of illness.
• Charles Rosenberg. *The Care of Strangers: The Rise of the American Hospital System*. New York: Basic Books, 1987. A good treatment of how U.S. handles illness.
• Nancy Scheper-Hughes. *Death Without Weeping: The Violence of Everyday Life inBrazil*. Berkeley, CA: University of California Press, 1992. An excellent account of AIDS and other ills of the poor.

# A. Promoting Environmental Justice

PAULETTE V. WALKER

*Many areas of the U.S. have significant problems with air, water, and land pollution. The residents of these areas, though, are usually poor members of minority groups who live near dumps or polluted areas because of the need for cheap housing. This situation has drawn the attention of both civil rights groups and environmentalists and created a new concept called environmental racism. This reading reports on the work of one person trying to achieve environmental justice to protect residents of two black communities, one in Harlem and one in South Africa. It explains the situation created by severe pollution and points to efforts to create environmental justice.*

The similarities between Cape Town and New York City disturb Larry L. Rasmussen, a professor of social ethics at Union Theological Seminary here. "The poorest neighborhoods in both Cape Town and New York City are the most toxic, the most environmentally damaged," he says. "Look at West Harlem, in New York. City officials have put the sewage-treatment plant *and* the bus barns there-which exacerbates the pollution in the area. The city garbage trucks unload their trash there. And all of this next to a grade school."

"In Cape Town," he says, "the townships are located on the worst land. It's impossible for the residents to exist on what this land produces."

Mr. Rasmussen spent most of January in South Africa. While there, he met with community organizers and like-minded idealists at the University of Cape Town and the University of Western Cape to plan a bi-national coalition on "eco-social justice." This coalition, he says, will exchange ideas to help cities like Cape Town and New York deal with poverty, environmental racism, and ethnic divisiveness-conditions that undermine eco-social justice.

## SOCIETY AND THE ENVIRONMENT

Eco-social justice does not have a precise definition. Mr. Rasmussen says the movement is about more than the environment: It's about the equitable distribution of natural resources, and the way people from different backgrounds and economic classes treat one another.

"There's a connection between the health and well-being of human society, and the health and well-being of nature," Mr. Rasmussen says. "When resources are

*Reprinted from Paulette V. Walker, "Promoting Environmental Justice," THE CHRONICLE OF HIGHER EDUCATION, April 5, 1996, p. A7.*

exhausted, people suffer. When the society is a very unjust one, with major gaps between the rich and the poor, the world of nature is also negatively affected."

Such degradation, he says, has been going on since humans made the switch to agriculture from hunting and gathering 10,000 years ago. But continuing this habit of sacrificing nature for the sake of society, he says, will eventually destroy the planet's life support system.

"The present course is unsustainable," he says. "How do we get from the unsustainable present to the sustainable future?" He offers an answer to that question in his book Earth Community, Earth Ethic, to be published this fall by Orbis Books. In the book, he says that the agricultural, industrial, and informational revolutions "reorganized society so as to produce more effectively," but also "reconfigured nature for the sake of society."

To reverse the damage, he says there must be a fourth revolution one that will teach society how to be more like nature, where the waste from one organism becomes food for the next.

For example, in Kalundborg, a small city in Denmark, the power plant's excess steam is given to the oil refinery and to the pharmaceutical company, where it's used for heat and as a source of power for equipment.

The oil refinery uses the water a second time as a coolant for its refining process. The surplus gas produced from the refining process is stripped of sulfur and sold to the sheetrock factory and power plant. The sulfur is sold to the chemical company; the factory also uses some of the sulfur as a substitute for the mineral, gypsum. The ash generated from the burned coal is used to build roads.

## WORK IN HARLEM

Big cities also can be scenes of ecological and

social justice, he says. He offers, as an example, Bernadette Kosar, a Harlem community activist who works with teenagers to clear vacant lots and then plant gardens. She also visits grade schools to plant gardens on small plots in the play areas.

Then she teaches the kids about soil, gardening, and protecting the neighborhood," Mr. Rasmussen says. "Pretty soon, it's not just the kids who care about the garden, but the people in the neighborhood. They become protective of it, volunteer their time to keep it up. So in the end she has not only provided a green space, but she's provided a community-building project."

Kalundborg's changes were on a larger scale, Mr. Rasmussen says. But the idea-there in New York, and in Cape Town is to make the necessary incremental changes in a community "from the bottom up." Union Theological could have tried this approach with any number of countries, but Mr. Rasmussen says Union has had a relationship with South Africa since the 1960s, when Union students-in protest of apartheid-initiated the first boycott against American banks that were lending money to the South African government.

## SHARING INFORMATION

As part of the new effort, the University of Cape Town will share with Union the results of a study to explore what the churches in South Africa can do to end the ecological degradation in rural and urban parts of the country.

A representative from Harlem Initiatives Together, a community group of which Union is a member, will travel this spring to South Africa to share the group's programs with community activists there.

Barney Pityana, South Africa's Human Rights Commissioner, and Stanley Mahoba, a South African Methodist minister, will visit Union this month to discuss urban social and environmental issues.

Officials at Union are leading a project to incorporate the shared information into curriculum changes at Union and at the two universities in South Africa.

"So what we've got going," he says, "is an ongoing exchange of research, and an exchange of information with a view toward what is the proper action to be taken to address the social and environmental degradation in both places."

# B. Are Mega-Cities Viable?

EXEQUIEL EZCURRA AND MARISA MAZARI-HIRIART

*The growth of cities in Third World countries has reshaped the economies and politics, and created huge problems in these nations. Hundreds of thousands of people live on the streets, crime and rebellion soars, and pollution becomes a major headache. This reading describes one such "mega-city" in Mexcio which has grown by 1990 to over 15 million people and faces huge population and environmental overload.*

Rural Populations' "rush to the cities" has dramatically reshaped the landscape of Third World countries in the second half of this century. The phenomenon of urban concentration itself is not new, but the growth and development of large cities in the nonindustrialized world present a number of new characteristics that merit careful study. The first and perhaps most noticeable of these is centralism. Urbanization in the developed world was characterized by the growth of a large number of medium-sized cities. In the Third World, urban growth has been concentrated in or near a few very large cities, frequently referred to as "megalopolises." The megalopolis is a twentieth-century phenomenon. It is not yet clear how environmentally sustainable these cities will prove to be.

The world's population in 1995 is estimated as 5.67 billion, and it is increasing by some 100 million annually. By the year 2000, the majority of the world's people will be living in urban areas. But only 4 or 21 cities whose populations are expected to exceed 10 million inhabitants are located in countries whose per capita gross national product (GNP) exceeds $10,000 (U.S.). Furthermore, there is a significant inverse relationship between GNP and population growth rate in these megalopolises. The large cities of the poorer countries are actually growing much faster than similar cities in the industrialized world. Such unbridled growth puts a heavy economic burden on Third World urban conglomerates. Resource shortages are exacerbated by ever-increasing demands for services that need to be supplied at a rate that often exceeds economic growth. Air and water quality, environmentally-related health problems, water, food, and energy supply, and the risk of large-scale regional solid and liquid-waste contamination are all important problems faced by the megalopolis. They have yet to be addressed and resolved in a sustainable manner.

*Excerpted from Exequiel Ezcurra and Marisa Mazari-Hiriart, "Are Mega-Cities Viable?" ENVIRONMENT, January/February, 1996, pp. 8-14.*

Mexico City, one of the largest megalopolises on Earth, serves as the focus of an examination of the question of environmental sustainability. Mexico City is in one sense an ongoing experiment. Final conclusions about its environmental sustainability and economic sustainability and economic feasibility have yet to be drawn. The problems Mexico City faces are similar to those faced by many Third World megalopolises. Thus, its future is in part a clue to theirs.

The urban and demographic growth of the Basin of Mexico (the geographic area encompassing Mexico City) represents one of the main worries for environmentalists. The possible consequences of such an immense population concentration and its asymmetric relation to the rest of the nation accounts for part of this concern. The ecological consequences of approximately 18 million people occupying the same space are another factor. The foreshadowings for natural resource use are ominous. In the eyes of many, the enormity of such growth foreshadows a great ecological catastrophe that will lead to the compulsory decentralization of the megalopolis. Others see the urban concentration as the logical result of industrial development and twentieth-century technological progress and do not view the megalopolis as a problem in itself. In their minds, technological development will provide the solutions to the environmental and health problems created by such unrestrained urban growth. Clearly, an environmental crisis situation in Mexico City will almost certainly be generated by the exhaustion of the water supply, the degradation of the air, the silting up of the drainage system, and citywide flooding resulting from deforestation.

The population of Mexico City has long been the subject of debate. The last official census recorded the city's population as 15 million in 1990. This statistic seems unrealistic, however, when the growth of the urbanized area during the 1980s and the historic trends in population growth rates are taken into account. The present size of the urbanized area, as estimated by remote sensing techniques suggests a total population of about 16.8 million in 1990 and 18.5 million in 1995. Between 1950 and 1980, Mexico City's average annual growth was 4.8 percent. The continuous arrival of migrants from economically depressed rural areas accounts for much of the high growth rate. Between 1950 and 1980, 5.43 million immigrants arrived in Mexico City. However, between 1970 and 1980 alone, 3.25 million immigrants made their way to Mexico City. Assuming that a population of 18 million in 1995 is correct, the growth rate for the 1980s was around 1.8 percent, markedly lower than the rates for the previous decades. Only slightly denser than Tokyo or Caracas, Mexico City presently duplicates the densities of New York, Sao Paulo, and Buenos Aires. It has three times the density of Paris and four times that of London. Only some Asian cities like Bombay, Calcutta, and Hong Kong have higher population densities.

As Mexico City expanded, it did not replicate the old patterns of urbanization. The new developments are more dense, less planned, and generally include less open space. Many developments are now built on hillsides, generating a considerable amount of soil erosion and a significant increase in runoff and flash floods after rainstorms. In 1950, the urban area included a large proportion of agro-pastoral fields, together with numerous empty lots, parks, and public spaces. The relative frequency of these open spaces within the city has decreased considerably with the new industrial style of urbanization.

Although most of the environmental problems in the Basin of Mexico have reached critical proportions in the late 20th century, industrial development is not solely to blame. Urban and political centralism have been a tradition in Mexican society since the Aztec empire. Modern industrialization, however, has exaggerated this trend to dramatic proportions, and is indeed responsible for the disproportionate urbanization and the biased distribution of population and wealth. Although population growth in the basin is clearly decelerating, natural resource use is already highly unsustainable with the current population density. Fossil fuel consumption, the number of cars, deforestation, and the pumping of groundwater from a critically depleted aquifer are all increasing at a rate that often exceeds that of population growth.

In the past, resource exhaustion through improper land use has produced large declines in population, showing that there are limits to population growth in a closed basin with a given technological level. Air pollution, water shortages, the urban area's unbridled growth, and the ever-increasing economic and natural resource costs of maintaining the megalopolis suggest that a similar process of population limitation or even decline may occur in the future. In Mexico City, the use of air, water, and soils as a commons is clearly unsustainable, and the city's residents may soon confront hard and painful decisions. In our opinion, it is clear that in the future the subsidies will have to be eliminated and that the cost of living and the quality of life in the city will worsen. Government authorities have made several attempts over the past six years to set the price of water closer to its real cost, but popular protests have aborted these initiatives. However, the capacity to subsidize water use is becoming more and more constrained and will soon reach a limit.

Health problems typical of developed societies (like heart disease and malignant tumors) coexist with problems related to air and water pollution (such as pneumonia and enteritis) that are more typical of the developing world. Although there is no data on this problem, Mexico City's decreasing growth rates suggest that for some sectors of the population emigrating outside the basin into medium-sized cities is already an advantageous alternative.

Growing conflicts over water use, air pollution, waste disposal, environmentally related health problems, and natural resource depletion are all problems shared by most Third World megalopolises. Mexico City is thus a laboratory where many of the processes that drive population, natural resource, and land-use changes in the less-developed nations are being tested. It provides both fascinating and terrible insights into what the future may hold for many of the megalopolises of Latin America and the Third World.

# Resource Page

## A. PROMOTING ENVIRONMENTAL JUSTICE

### Study Questions

• What are some of the types of environmental injustices that exist in Harlem and Cape Town, South Africa?
• Why do poor neighborhoods suffer more environmental problems than other areas?
• What is eco-social justice, and how does the reading propose to implement it?
• How does environmental injustice relate to racial and economic injustice?
• What kind of large-scale social changes could end environmental injustice in both the U.S. and South Africa?

### Key Concepts

ecological degradation
eco-social justice
environmental racism
ethnic divisiveness
toxic

### Additional Resources

• Lester R. Brown. *State of the World.* New York: W. W. Norton, 1996. This report, which is published annually, provides updates on the environmental state of the world.
• Michael Edelstein. *Contaminated Communities: The Social and Psychological Impacts of Residential Toxic Exposure.* Boulder, CO: Westview Press, 1988. A study of the damage done by pollution.
• Murray Feshbach and Alfred Friendly. *Exocide in the USSR.* New York: Basic Books, 1992. The USSR is probably the most polluted area of the world, which this book documents.
• Larry L. Rasmussen. *Earth Community, Earth Ethic.* New York: Orbis Books, 1966. The article's author's basic work.
• W. Edward Stead and Jean Garner Stead. *Management for a Small Planet.* Newbury Park, CA: Sage, 1992. Some practical ideas for business to protect the environment.

## B. ARE MEGA-CITIES VIABLE?

### Study Questions

• What are some reasons why mega-cities have developed in Third World countries like Mexico?
• What problems do these large cities face today?
• What happens when a city's water supply and air quality are overwhelmed by overuse?
• How does the growth of these cities compare to urbanization in the U.S.?
• How can Third World governments act to solve the problems of mega-cities?

### Key Concepts

ecological consequences
environment
mega-cities
megalopolis
urban area

### Additional Resources

• Frances Fitzgerald. *Cities on a Hill.* New York: Simon & Schuster, 1987. A Pulitzer Prize-winning book on city culture.
Oscar Lewis. *The Children of Sanchez.* New York: Random House, 1961. An ethnography of city life in Mexico.
• Lewis Mumford. *The City In History.* New York: Harcourt, Brace, Jovancovich, 1961. The classic statement on the history of cities.
• Kirpatrick Sale. *Human Scale.* New York: Coward, McCall, & Geohegan, 1980. A book of proposals on designing cities on a smaller scale.
•Nancy Wiegersma. *Urban Leviathan: Mexico City in the Twentieth Century.* Philadelphia: Temple University Press, 1994. Background on Mexico City.

# A. The Global Tide

GEORGE A. LOPEZ, JACKIE G. SMITH AND RON PAGNUCCO

*Social movements and social change now occur all over the world, and have led to a greater interdependence of all people. These trends are called globalization, which is based on technology and rapid movement around the globe. This article describes these changes as part of a "global tide" which is transforming the world in positive and negative ways. The hope for peace and cooperation is great, but globalization increases tensions and the potential for conflict.*

In the 1970s, babies in Third World nations were dying when they might have been thriving. The apparent culprit: ersatz mother's milk made from powder. The Nestle Company, a Swiss-based multinational, had identified Third World mothers as a high-growth marketing opportunity. Nestle baby formula was aggressively pushed as the "modern" way to feed infants.

In the developed world, baby formula works fine. It may not be as good as mother's milk, but it's reasonably close. As long as the bottles and rubber nipples for the formula are properly sterilized, the mixing water reasonably pure, and the mixing proportions right, babies do well on it.

But in Third World villages in the 1970s, pure water was the exception, not the rule, and the need for sterilization was hard to explain and seldom practiced. Beyond that, the formula was cheap by First World standards, but expensive by Third World reckonings. That made it fatally tempting to stretch the powder by diluting it too much, thus degrading the nutritional value.

Health care professionals and missionaries working in the Third World were outraged, and they communicated their sadness and anger to Nestle, which did nothing, and to governments, which didn't seem to care. Nestle had threatened no nation's security, broken no laws.

But nutritionists and activists in the industrialized world did care, and condemnation of Nestle's marketing practices became widespread. As word got out, the cause was taken up by nearly 100 private organizations in 65 nations. A transnational economic boycott of Nestle products was launched, coordinated by a U.S.-based transnational citizen coalition, the Infant Formula Action Committee (INFACT).

Whether the boycott had much economic effect

*Excerpted from George A. Lopez, Jackie G. Smith, and Ron Pagnucco, "The Global Tide," THE BULLETIN OF THE ATOMIC SCIENTISTS, July/August, 1995, pp. 33 ff.*

on Nestle's bottom line is hard to pin down. But it became a public relations nightmare for a company that liked to be known for its warm and cuddly hot chocolate and its candy-counter Crunch bars. The INFACT-led transnational campaign ultimately forced Nestle to abandon its Third World marketing practices, and it also led to the passage in 1981 of a World Health Organization code of conduct governing the marketing and sale of infant formula.

The Nestle boycott was arguably the first activist campaign of its type. It attracted cross-border participants who organized outside traditional diplomatic or political channels in an attempt to accomplish reform in an area outside the immediate interests of international politics. The success of the boycott, and the apparent influence of two other transnational movements of the early 1980s-the campaign against the deployment of intermediate-range missiles in Europe and the divestment campaign to end apartheid in South Africa-have inspired citizen groups around the world to organize around common cross-national interests.

Transnational social movements are one aspect of "globalization"—a term pundits use to describe the rapidly increasing cross-border economic, social, and political interactions that are not originated by national governments. Although theorists argue about when the trend toward globalization began, few would deny that the process has been accelerating for more than two decades.

It was in the 1970s that Americans discovered-with a jolt-that the world's economy had become highly interdependent. In 1971, President Richard Nixon withdrew the dollar from the gold standard. From then on, the dollar floated against other currencies, thus facilitating—in theory—worldwide free trade.

When the Organization of Petroleum Exporting Countries (OPEC) restricted oil production and distribution in 1973, it sent a series of shock waves through Western economies. The OPEC oil embargo demonstrated that the Western nations had become shockingly vulnerable to external pressure, and their governments could do little about it.

At first, only the economies of advanced industrial states were thought to be closely inter-connected, but when the entire world felt the effects of the debt crises in developing countries in the post-OPEC world, opinions were revised.

Danish analysts Hans-Henrik Holm and Georg Sorensen define globalization as the intensification of economic, social, and political interaction across national boundaries. Noting the dramatic increase that has occurred in both the breadth and depth of across-bor-der activity, they label the 1970s the decade of interdependence, and the 1980s the decade of intensification.

Superpower detente was one of the conditions that favored the increase in transnational activities that began in the mid-1970s. International contacts were no longer limited to diplomats or globe-trotting businessmen. And many of the issues that stimulated new transnational associations went beyond the political-economic and military-security issues that states traditionally concerned themselves with.

In the social and political spheres, it was becoming clear that many modern social problems were not confined within boundaries, nor did ways of dealing with issues like human rights, refugees, and environmental concerns fit neatly with notions of national sovereignty. Many of those committed to solving modern social problems were citizen-activists unaffiliated with their governments.

In the 1980s, as national leaders continued to initiate state policies and administer them through traditional diplomatic avenues, a new and diverse set of international actors gradually made their appearance in matters of "low politics," as dealing with the environment, human rights, and related issues came to be called.

To Robert Keohane of Harvard University, "globalization is fundamentally a social process, not one that is technologically predetermined." Keohane argues that the global economy and the new communications technologies are necessary components of globalization, but they do not alone explain global social change. The critical component is the growing number of individuals with a transnational conscience who are committed to solving the pressing social and political problems of our age.

Globalization's greatest strength lies in its poten-tial to improve the economic, social, and political life of all people. But globalization should unfold in ways that allow local groups to participate as equal partners. They are the resident change agents who understand the opportunities and obstacles in their own local-global nexus.

One of the most compelling questions asked about globalization is whether it will lead to a truly global civil society, which many believe is the key to world peace. Both in reality and in its prescriptive allure, globalization is appealing. But its long-term consequences are the subject of spirited debate. Some predict that one outcome will be more direct democracy at the local level. Other analysts believe that globalization is already being counterbalanced by other forces. Rosenau asserts that globalization brings with it its own self-correcting, if not countervailing, tendencies, such as fragmentation and localism." For every pressure that pushes people to be or do the same things-to "act globally"—there is a distinctly local counterpressure. For example, the former superpowers and their citizens may seek new forms of global security, but local rivalries, hatreds and wars continue.

# B. Dawn of the Dragon Century

## FAR EASTERN ECONOMIC REVIEW

*The half-dozen Asian countries that now lead the world in economic growth have sometimes been called the "six drag-ons," because of their dedication to expansion. This metaphor descibes the great economic impact of Asia, and how they are seen by the rest of the world. This reading, which reviews several new books on Asia, projects the growth of Asian economies into the 21st century, and concluded that we are at the dawn of the "dragon century."*

What is happening in Asia is by far the most important development in the world. Nothing else comes close, not only for Asians but for the entire planet. The modernization of Asia will forever reshape the world as we move toward the next millennium.

In the 1990s Asia came of age. As we move toward the year 2000, Asia will become the dominant region of the world: economically, politically and culturally. We are on the threshold of the Asian Renaissance.

This is not a change the rest of the world will readily accept. Yet it is time for all of us to face reality. And to devise a strategy for change. Given the extraordinary changes in the works, it is high time for the West to try to see the world from Asia's perspective. In Asia, for example, it is widely believed that the West is losing moral standing internationally, as shown in its lack of leadership in the crisis in Bosnia-Herzegovina. Given this perception, Asians are increasingly irritated by the West's lecturing and hectoring on freedom and human rights.

America's moralizing may come back to haunt it. Down the road imagine a big, economically powerful China threatening to withhold Most-Favoured-Nation status from the U.S. unless it did something about the slums in its big urban centers (or improved those SAT scores!).

A new network of nations based on economic symbiosis is emerging: the Asian network. With a spirit of working together for mutual economic gain, a new Asian collaboration is emerging in Asia for the first time. The catalyst is the free market.

The old Asia was divided by culture, language, political ideology, religious philosophies and geography. The new Asia, forged by economic integration, technology-especially telecommunications-travel and mobility of people, increasingly looks like one coherent region. In the 1960s young people in Europe began for the first time to call themselves Europeans, rather than English, French, German, just as many young people throughout Asia are beginning to call themselves Asians.

Up until the 1990s everything revolved around the West. The West set the rules. Japan was run by those rules during its economic emergence. But now Asians-the rest of Asia-are creating rules and will soon determine the game as well. Even Japan will be left behind as the countries of Southeast Asia, led by the overseas Chinese and China, increasingly hold economic sway.

As far as Hong Kong is concerned it sometimes seems as if Westerners think China is stealing a little Eurpoean outpost. Hong Kong is China.

Peking changed its name to Beijing; Saigon became Ho Chi Minh City; Burma became Myanmar. Just recently, Bombay was renamed Mumbai. How many people in the West took notice? These are symbolic changes, and we will have more of them When Macau returns to China at the end of this decade, the final chapter of Western dominance will have been written. For the first time in 400 years, every inch of Asian soil will be controlled and managed by Asians.

The modernization of Asia must not be thought of as the Westernization of Asia, but the modernization of Asia in the "Asian Way."

At the same time as Asia is modernizing, the Asian conscience is rising. It is very much the Asianization of Asia. In the past a young Indonesian travelling in the West, if asked where she was from, would have said "Indonesia." Today, more likely than not, she would say Asia."

The West needs the East a lot more than the East needs the West.

The Asian continent, from India to Japan, from below the old Soviet Union down to Indonesia, now accounts for more than half of the world's population. Within five years or less, more than half of these Asian house-

*Excerpted from "Dawn of the Dragon Century," FAR EASTERN ECONOMIC REVIEW, November 16, 1995, pp. 80-82.*

holds will be able to buy an array of consumer goods-refrigerators, television sets, washing machines, computers, cosmetics, etc. And as many as half a billion will be what the West understands as middle class. That market is roughly the size of the U.S. and Europe combined. As the widely placed Hongkong Bank advert says, "There are 3 billion people in Asia. Half of them are under 25. Consider it a growing market." This is a consumer miracle holding vast economic consequences.

Many Asians have told me that they believe in the long run they will beat the West competitively because they do not have and will not have a social-security system, or any of the other manifestations of the welfare state. Yet this is an economic factor most Westerners have completely closed their eyes to. What does it mean, particularly in economic terms?

In Asian families take care of themselves, above all else, and personal responsibility is emphasized. For Asians, the very idea of a central government being involved in family life is culturally unthinkable, horrifying. The concept of taking care of family first is why the savings rate in Asia is 30% or more than in almost every country. Asia lives out family values and self-sufficiency.

Not only do Asians believe the cost of the welfare state is a heavy burden on competitiveness, they also contend that it undermines the importance of family and leads to out-of-wedlock children (in the U.S. 30% of children are born out of wedlock, while in Malaysia it is 2%), high divorce rates, crime, loss of self-reliance and lower academic achievement.

This raises central questions for the West, especially for the U.S. and Europe. Are our welfare states now burdening our global competitiveness to a point where we must make some changes? Have they undermined the self-reliance of our citizens? Has our noble experiment failed? It is, I think, important to notice that today every country in the West, including the United States, is trying to cut back on welfare state excesses.

What can Asia teach the West and its young people? Buried under the collapsed department store in Seoul for 10 days, 20 year-old Korean Choi Myong Sok became a youth hero in his country. Businesses were eager to cash in on his image of courage with lucrative media offers. But Choi would have none of it. "They don't understand my pain," he said. "They just want to make money. I don't believe in that." Can Asia's philosophy and teachings help to spark off a global moral renaissance, led by Asians?

In the West the least understood Asian phenomenon is the role of the Overseas Chinese who live outside the mainland of China, not only in Taiwan, Hong Kong and Singapore, but also those in Indonesia, the Philippines, Malaysia, Thailand, and in Vancouver and Los Angeles and London. The most successful entrepreneurs in the world, they are the force that will catapult Asia to economic dominance. Paradoxes abound. BMW is now assembling cars in Vietnam, paying its auto workers $1 a day, while the hotels of Asia's cities (including Saigon and Hanoi) are among the most expensive in the world. Fifty years from now, it will be clear that the most momentous global development of the 1990s and the early part of the 21st century was the modernization of Asia.

Built on exports, Asian economies will increasingly be fuelled by consumer spending and, with it, the emerging middle class. By the year 2000, Asia will have almost half a billion people who are what we generally understand as middle class.

For the Chinese, the year 2000 is the year of the dragon, the year that will usher in the Dragon Century. John Hung, an expatriate Westerner who has lived for a long time in Hong Kong, points to a critical difference between Eastern and Western societies.

"A bus driver looking from his window at a passing Rolls-Royce says to himself, full of hope, 'I may not sit in that car, but my son will.'" In contrast, Hung adds; Westerners have a strong entitlement mentality. They insist on their rights "whereas Asians aspire."

# Resource Page

## A. THE GLOBAL TIDE

### Study Questions

• What is meant by "globalization" and what is an example of it?
• Why does globalization lead to interdependence and intensification?
• What kinds of social problems are created by the massive changes promoted by globalization?
• How have computers helped stimulate globalization?
• How might these globalizing trends shape the future of the U.S.?

### Key Concepts

intensification
interdependence
globalization
nationalism
multinational corporations

### Additional Resources

• Mike Featherstore (ed.). *Global Culture: Globalization, Nationalism, and Modernity.* Newbury Park, CA: Sage, 1990. Essays on the new global culture.
• William B. Johnston and Arnold E. Packer. *Workforce 2000: Work and Workers for the Twenty-First Century. Indianapolis:* Hudson Institute, 1987. An effort to look at the new shape of workers.
• Paul M. Kennedy. *The Rise and Fall of the Great Powers.* New York: Random House, 1988. A provocative look at why many great countries, including the U.S., might fall by the wayside.
• David C. Korten. *Getting to the 21st Century: Voluntary Action and the Global Agenda.* West Hartford, CT: Kumarian Press, 1990. A handbook on grass roots activism from a global perspective.
• Joel Mokay. *The Lever of Riches: Technological Creativity and Economic Progress.* New York: Oxford University Press, 1991. A treatment of technology and the future.

## B. DAWN OF THE DRAGON CENTURY

### Study Questions

• What countries make up the Asian economic movement?
• How do Asian nations work together to promote incredible economic growth?
• Why does the article's author feel that these nations will make up the "dragon century"?
• What might be the impact of this growth on the economic and political status of the U.S.?
• What problems might this new dragon century create for the world?

### Key Concepts

Asia
dragon century
modernization
government-driven economy
market-driven economy

### Additional Resources

• Nuala Beck. Shifting Gears: *Thriving in the New Economy.* New York: HarperCollins, 1995. Suggestions on how to take advantage of new economic forces.
• Peter Berger. *The Capitalist Revolution: Fifty Propositions about Prosperity, Equality, and Liberty.* New York: Basic Books, 1986. A good look at the impact of capitalism on society.
• John Naisbitt. *Megatrends Asia.* London: Nicholas Brealy Publishing, 1996. An analysis of Asia's future by an experienced analysts.
• Jim Rohwer. *Asia Rising.* Singapore: Butterworth-Heinemann, 1996. An interpretive view of Asia's future.
• Tomotsu Sengoku. *Willing Workers: The Work Ethics in Japan, England, and the United States.* Westport, CT: Quorum Books, 1985. This excellent comparison shows why Asian workers are more productive.